Haitian Eyes, Haitian Hands

© 2015 by Biola University Journalism Department
Published by Biola Avenue Press
Biola University, 13800 Biola University Drive,
La Mirada, CA 90639

Printed in the United States of America

Cover photo by Alissa Sandoval

ISBN 978-0-9839572-4-9

Request for information should be addressed to:

Dr. Tamara J. Welter, Journalism & Integrated Media Department
Biola University, 13800 Biola University, La Mirada, CA 90639

Table of Contents

Introduction

Dearest Reader:

When we started this book, we wanted to tell the Haitian story. We quickly realized that everyone wanted to tell the Haitian story. All the foreign voices from around the world drown out the Haitian voices that cry out. Our hands and eyes reveal powerful things about who we are as people. The posture of our hands and the activities they perform are expressions of our hearts' motivations, beliefs and desires. The eyes, as the saying goes, are the windows to our souls. The purpose of highlighting the two was to expand our vision and the vision of our readers—to see with the eyes of a Haitian; to understand their hearts through the postures of their hands. We will always be somewhat removed from these people that we have grown to love in the previous few months. With the help of a young Haitian writer named Larsen and a few Haitian photographers from the New Missions School in Léogâne—who offered up their hands and gave us a glimpse of the world through their eyes—we have in some small way accomplished our goal.

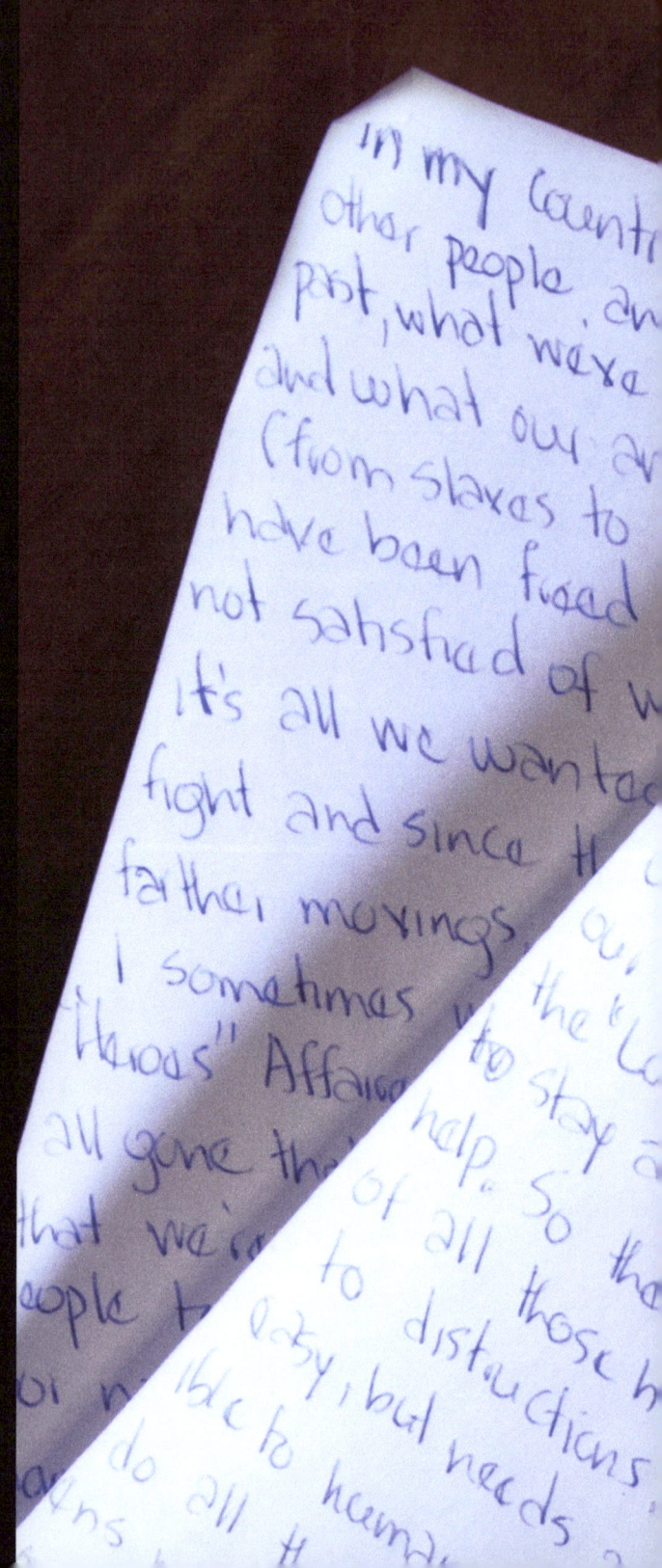

all are p...
...ing them...
...thru, ho...
...s or...

Many People of great knowledge and with working hands and brains not trusting any bad spirits (voodoo) to Protect empir... little bad People's eyes on them or with blind faith in God won't dare to attemp the Presidency or being candidate at any institution or work. No one would do so without having or laying on a strong Powerful protector. Most of the times I lay on yoodoo or bad spirits which they think or called "cultural abrations" and think normal...

I think is when we trust in human spirits to come and take Part in projects. We're just telling G... above all" and the most Pow... and that we don't... So lution...

God's ... Our lives ... we need. God Plays a Big Par... most necessary part in... ment or success. I'm su... to him then to vood... which caese us... and sisters a... them as... Stop Pa... G...

Free Hands

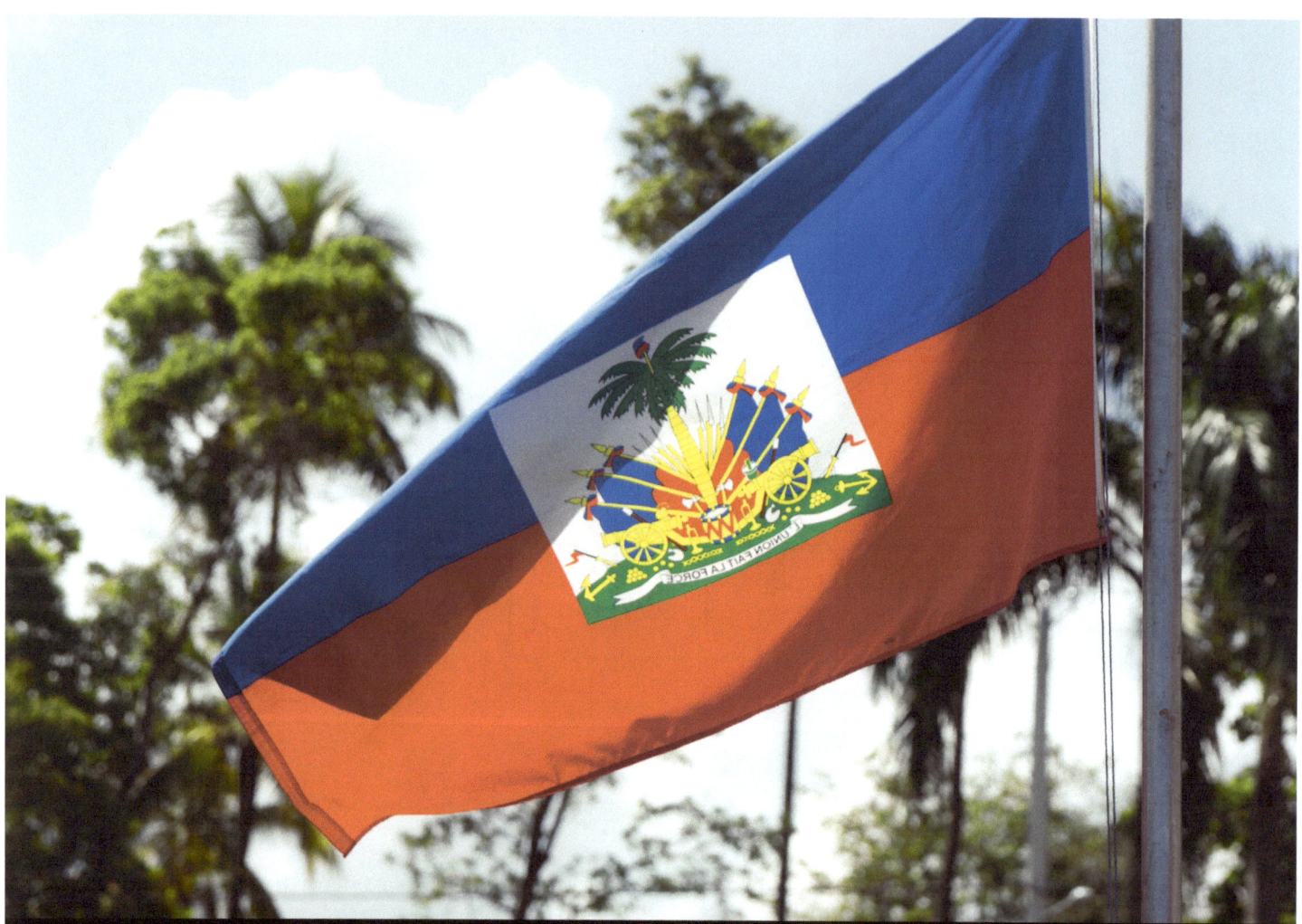

"In my country, we are all proud of telling other people and hearing them talk about our past—what we've been through, how we survived and what our ancestors or heroes made possible [from slaves to free people]. [They] have fought and have been freed from slavery, but yet still not satisfied of what we're seeing. Seem like it's all we wanted, for we've stopped the fight and since then there haven't been any further movings, efforts and determination. I sometimes wonder, "Was it just a hero" or "heroes" affair or work, and because they've all gone that their time has passed...and that we're left with no such determined people to do the following steps for that poor nation."

- Larson

Chapter 1
History

Haitians were introduced to the world in shackles.

At the time, the island was a French colony owned by the French West India Company, a booming and successful industry in the Western World. Nicknamed the "Pearl of Antilles" due to its overflowing wealth, it gained the title as one of the richest colonies in the 18th century by the French Empire. By the 1780s, the island produced near 40 percent of sugar and 60 percent of coffee consumed in Europe. In fact, this one colony produced more sugar and coffee than all of Britain's West Indian Colonies combined.

Therefore, it is natural to understand that this colony needed a vast number of workers—with such a high demand from the rest of the world. This specific workforce was made up of imported African slaves—790,000 in the 1780s to be more specific. This number made up one third of the entire Atlantic slave trade. And this large number of slaves was ruled over by a population of white colonists who made up not even ten percent of the African population.

The breaking point that led to the revolution was built on a long and enduring foundation of extremely oppressive and harsh treatment that was instigated by *Code Noire*, which allowed certain rights to slaves and responsibilities to the master that included food, clothes and general well being. At the same time, this code also allowed for brutal methods of punishment to stamp a forced obedience into the wills of the slaves. One such slave, who later became the personal secretary of Henri Christophe, the president of Haiti in the turn of the 19th century, described the unimaginable crimes enacted against the slaves by their French owners including extreme forms of torture that would seem unbelievable in today's world:

"Have they not put men and women inside barrels studded with spikes and rolled them down mountainsides into the abyss? Have they not consigned these miserable blacks to man-eating dogs until the latter, sated by human flesh, left the mangled victims to be finished off with bayonet and poniard?"

With a ratio of 10 slaves to every one colonist in 1790 and the horrific treatment slaves received, a revolution was inevitable and a revolution did happen. But the unfolding of the drama began with a dispute between two groups of people—and neither group consisted of slaves.

In the late 18th century, Vincent Oge, a wealthy mixed-race man, traveled to France and demanded that the government recognize mixed-race Haitians as French citizens with the full range of rights. After his demands were denied, he created a rebellion that quickly fizzled out because of the mixed-race peoples' refusal to arm and/or free their slaves for the cause. While Oge was captured and executed in 1791, the age of rebellion was just beginning.

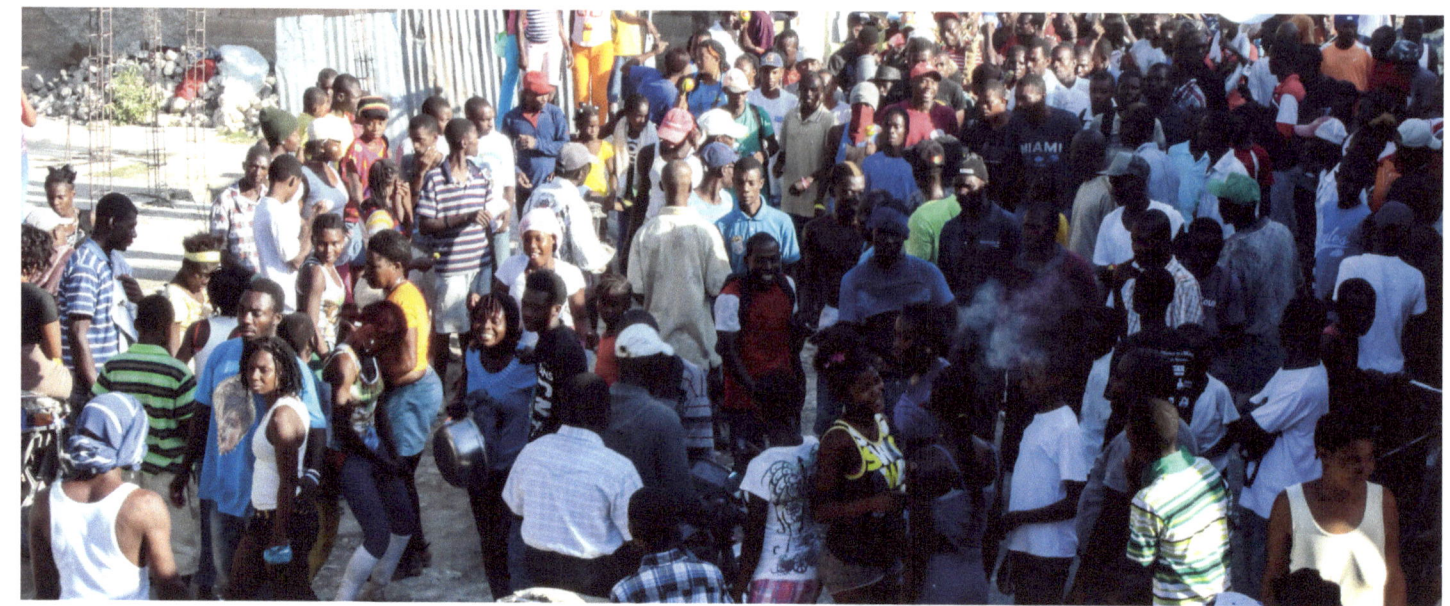

What Oge's revolt provided to the slaves was an advantage of distraction. The fighting among classes in Haiti in combination with the French Revolution, hid the plotting occurring among slaves, according to Alex Dupuy, native born and educated Haitian and professor of sociology at Wesleyan University. This tension was largely stirred up by an unlikely hero: a voodoo priest, Dutty Boukman. Boukman led a call to arms in 1791 and the slaves took the call in great strides. Northern plantations were burnt to the ground and the fury raged throughout the land swiftly.

Léger-Félicité Sonthonax, a radically forward-thinking French civil commissioner who was also an abolitionist, was immediately sent to the French colony in order to maintain French control on the island and ensure the social equality that was granted to the free people of color. He took this a step further by proclaiming all slaves in the north province as free men. This radical move led to the French National Convention three years later eventually abolishing slavery in France and all of its colonies in 1794.

As one would expect, such a radical turn led to backlash from white colonists and also from many free men of color. The British, usually an enemy of France, stepped in to oppose the abolition of slavery. However, under the military leadership of Toussaint Louverture, a freed slave with organized and shrewd military tactics, the British were driven out by 1801. He was able to gain control of a large portion of the island and it was through his actions that Louverture was dubbed the "father of Haiti."

Louverture did not proclaim full independence for the country, but it was enough independence for Napoleon Bonaparte to send a massive invasion force in order to increase French control. With the French general Toussa Rochambeau leading Napoleon's forces, the struggle turned cruel with excessive amounts of blood spilt on both sides. Eventually, the tide turned in favor of the former slaves as Napoleon became preoccupied with the war in Europe and the Louisiana Purchase. The Haitian Army, led by Jean Jacques Dessalines, defeated Rochambeau and the French Army in 1803.

Dessalines, the new self-elected emperor, declared independence for Haiti and the chains were finally broken.

As the French fled to Louisiana or Cuba, those remaining were slaughtered by Haitian military forces in a moment that is remembered with pride by Haitians today. Dessalines proclaimed these powerful words that ring among the ears of Haitians today:

"We have repaid these cannibals, war for war, crime for crime, outrage for outrage."

Haiti found its independence in a similar way to the United States.

"History is a source of pride for most Haitians because unlike many other parts of the colonial world, Haiti won its independence much like the United States did by revolting against colonial power," said Dupuy.

And yet, Haiti holds a unique and significant weight of pride to their specific revolution in that not only did it gain them independence, but it combated an oppressive racial system that had been established in years before.

"Neither the American revolution nor the French Revolution wanted to abolish slavery or the system of racial oppression or racial apartheid so the Haitian revolution was a blow to that ideology and that system," said Dupuy.

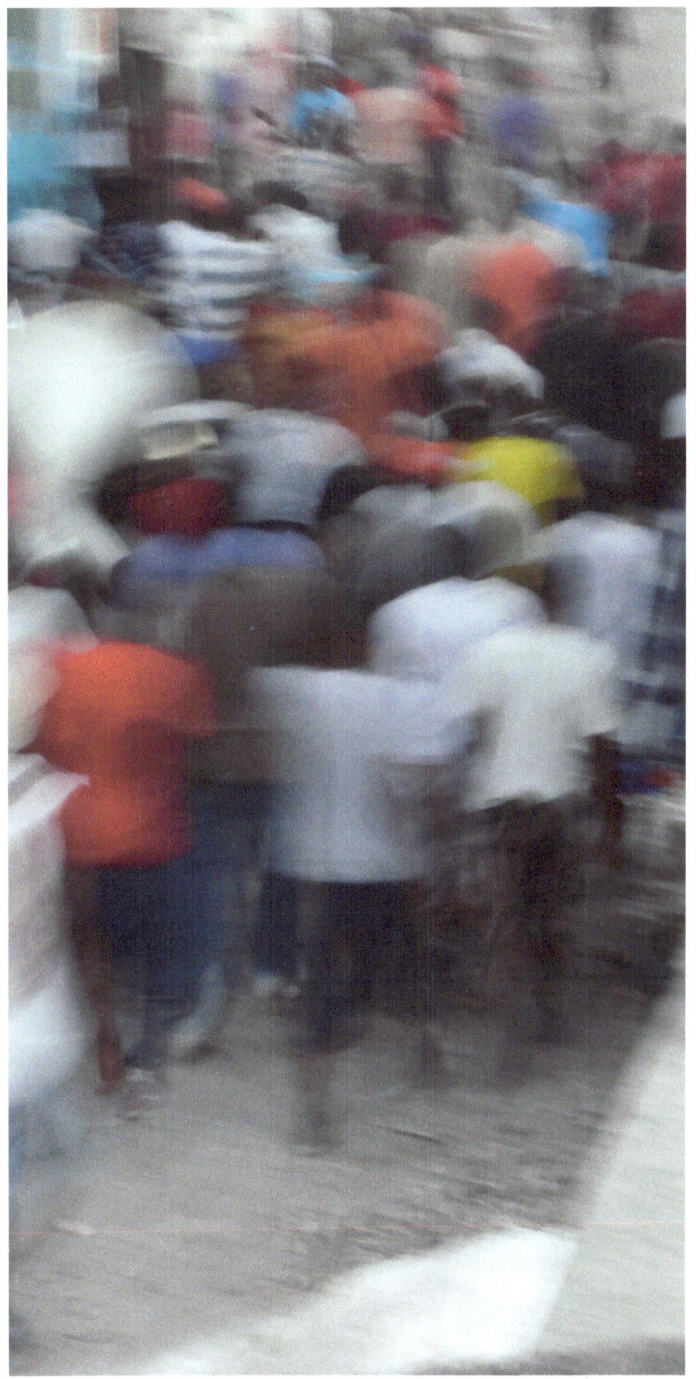

Photo // Jean-Jacques Hosellio

2/7/91: Reverend Jean Bertrand-Aristide becomes Haiti's first democratically elected president

10/15/94: President Aristide returns to Haiti and to power with the help of U.S. troops and UN sanctions after three years of exile.

12/23/95: Term limits prevent President Aristide from running again. His protege, Rene Preval, is elected to succeed him.

1/11/99: President Rene Preval announces plans to bypass parliamentary elections and appoint a new government by decree.

11/26/00: Aristide runs for a second, nonconsecutive term and wins 92% of the vote. Major opposition parties boycott the election and allege corruption.

11/28/02: Thousands protest against President Aristide's administration, violently clashing with Aristide supporters in the streets.

1/1/04: Celebrations for Haiti's 200th anniversary of independence from France sparks unrest and dissatisfaction with Aristide's administration.

2/04: Violent clashes between protesters turn into widespread rebellion and bloody battles between guerilla troops and Haitian police forces.

2/29/04: President Aristide resigns and flees into exile in South Africa. Boniface Alexandre, Supreme Court Justice, takes over as interim president. American and UN troops arrive to restore order.

7/15/06: Thousands demonstrate to demand the return of exiled President Aristide.

4/12/08: Prime Minister Jacques Adouard Alexi is dismissed in an attempt to quell protests.

10/30/09: Lawmakers oust Prime Minister Michele Pierre-Louis and appoint Jean-Max Bellerive instead.

5/18/10: More than 2,000 demonstrators outside the national palace call for President Preval's resignation.

1/12/10: A 7.0 earthquake hits Haiti, resulting in the deaths of more than 200,000. International task forces rush to Haiti to assist in the rescue and rebuilding effort.

5/19/09: Bill Clinton is appointed as the United Nations' special envoy to Haiti.

4/7-9/08: Hungry protestors storm the Presidential Palace demanding President's Preval's resignation due to high food prices.

2/15/06: Rene Preval is declared the winner of the presidential elections after an agreement between the interim government and the electoral council.

2/17/04: President Aristide makes a televised appeal for international help, saying his country is in the midst of a coup attempt.

1/7/04: University students protest against President Aristide, demanding his resignation.

4/3/03: Haiti's government officially sanctions voodoo as an official religion.

12/17/01: A coup led by ex-members of the disbanded military fails to oust President Aristide.

4/3/00: Radio journalist Jean Dominique is killed by gunmen in an assassination believed to be sanctioned by top government officials.

11/30/96: United Nations peacekeeping mandate in Haiti expires, but it extended for another year.

2/6/95: President Aristide disbands Haitian military and installs civilian police force

9/30/91: A coup led by Brigadier-General Raoul Cedras sends President Aristide and Prime Minister Rene Preval into exile, inciting diplomatic and trade sanctions from the United States and other countries around the world.

10/24/10: A cholera outbreak, which is eventually traced to UN troops and will kill thousands, begins.

12/8/10: Michel Martelly, a former singer and popular presidential candidate, urges his supporters to nonviolently protest the allegedly rigged election results which showed his apparent loss.

2/3/11: President Preval's chosen successor, Jude Celestin, is dropped from the election run-off. Martelly and former first lady Mirlande Manigat proceed to the run-off.

5/14/11: President Michel Martelly is officially sworn into office.

10/4/11: Gary Conille is approved as the Prime Minister, after President Martelly's previous two choices were rejected by Haitian lawmakers.

9-10/2012: Thousands protest in Port-au-Prince, demanding a lower cost of living and alleging corruption within President Martelly's administration.

1/17/14: The investigation into the assassination of radio journalist Jean Dominique in 2000 concludes, accusing several close associates of former President Aristide.

11/29/14: Young Haitians in several cities across the country stage demonstrations demanding the resignation of President Martelly.

1/11/15: More than 1500 people March against Martelly's government in streets of Port-au-Prince

1/15/15: President Martelly's appointee Evans Paul assumes office as Prime Minister.

2/10/15: Protests and strikes over fuel prices shutdown Port-au-Prince

2/2015: More than 6,000 marched in Port-au-Prince to demand lower gas prices & Martelly's resignation

4/17/15: Protesters in northeast Haiti demanding water, electricity and a lower cost of living.

3/15/15: The Haitian government announces that legislative elections will be held August 9 and presidential elections on October 25

2/18/15: A stampede at a carnival parade in Port-au-Prince kills 16 people and injures 78 more after onlookers flee falling power lines. Outraged citizens later blame Martelly's administration.

1/23-25/15: UN officials including US ambassador Samantha Power visited Haiti to evaluate plans to reduce UN presence and to urge elections.

1/12/15: President Martelly fails to reach an agreement with parliament regarding term extensions and election dates. Parliamentary members' terms end, leaving only 10 members in the Senate and none in the Chamber of Deputies.

12/14/14: Prime Minister Laurent Lamothe and his cabinet resign after crowds demanded government resignations and promised elections

11/18/14: Former President Aristide's political party leads the largest anti-government protests since 2011. Police fire tear gas to disperse crowds.

3/2013: Deaths from the cholera epidemic reach 8,000.

2/29/12: Supporters of former president Aristide rally in the Port-au-Prince on the eighth anniversary of his exile. Demonstrators accuse Martelly of not doing enough to help Haiti recover from the 2010 earthquake.

9/14/11: Haitian protesters call for the removal of UN troops.

3/20/11: Martelly wins the delayed elections with 68% of the vote.

12/14/10: Martelly's apparent loss in the November 28 elections spur days of rioting. Martelly calls for electoral college to be replaced and the vote redone with all original candidates.

11/28/10: Haiti holds presidential elections amid accusations of President Preval attempting to install his successor, Jude Celestin in flawed elections.

Worshiping Hands

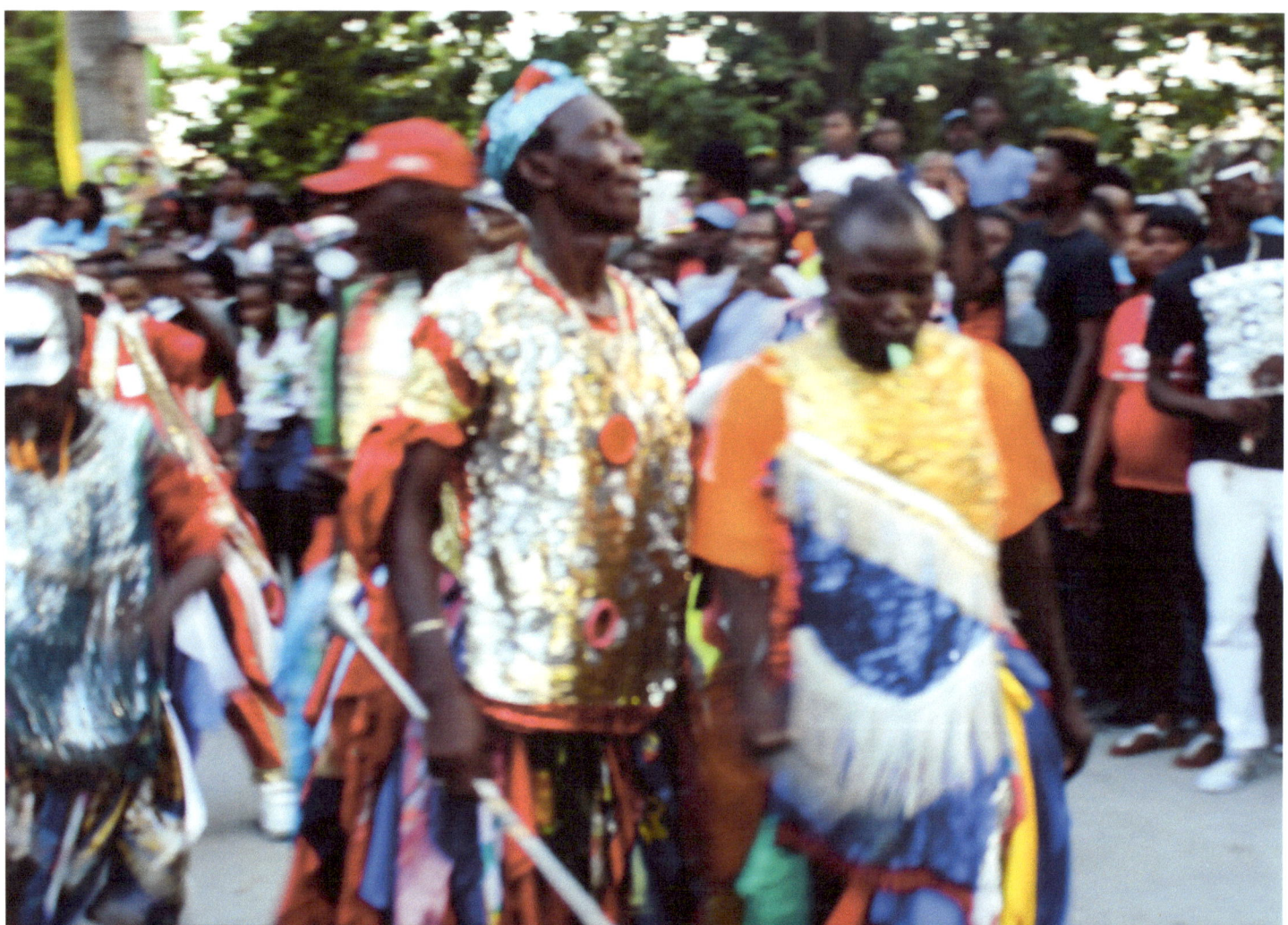

"When we trust in human or bad spirits to come and take part in our life and projects, we're just telling "God" the "Lord" "Above all" and the most powerful to stay away and that we don't need his help. So the best solution is to get rid of all those bad spirits which lead us to destructions. It will certainly not be easy, but needs a start. For what's impossible to human is possible with God."

- Larson

Photo // Holophene Thierry

Chapter 2
Haitian Voodoo

On the night of August 14, 1791, Haitian slaves gathered in the woods near the French colony of Saint-Domingue for a secret voodoo ceremony. The ceremony served as both a religious ritual and the first meeting to organize a revolt against the ruling class—the white French colonists of the wealthy Northern Plain. It was voodoo that united the slaves in their defiance. Their refusal to abandon their West African religious roots represented a rejection of what they perceived to be the god of the whites—whom they connected with the injustice they had endured at the hands of the French.

Dutty Boukman, their leader and a prominent houngan (voodoo priest), opened the ceremony with a prayer:

"Good Lord who hath made the sun that shines upon us, that riseth from the sea, who maketh the storm to roar; and governeth the thunders, The Lord is hidden in the heavens, and there He watcheth over us. The Lord seeth what the [whites] have done. Their god commandeth crimes, ours giveth blessings upon us. The Good Lord hath ordained vengeance. He will give strength to our arms and courage to our hearts. He shall sustain us. Cast down the image of the god of the [whites], because he maketh the tears to flow from our eyes. Hearken unto Liberty that speaketh now in all your hearts" (translated from Haitian Creole).

The mambo (voodoo priestess) Cécile Fatiman slit the throat of a black Creole pig as a sacrifice to Ezili Dantor, the "mother of Haiti." Rallied to anger, the slaves drank the pig's blood and swore a sacred oath to overthrow their French masters.

One week later, they fulfilled their vow. Roughly one thousand slaves rebelled simultaneously. The air was filled with ashes as plantations and farms were set aflame. White slaveholders and their families were massacred. For over a decade, Haiti was ravaged by one of the bloodiest periods in human history until the Haitians finally gained their independence on January 1, 1804—making it the first black republic the world had ever seen.

A Way of Life

Haiti's story cannot be understood apart from voodoo.

While the impoverished Caribbean island has been associated with many things—desperation, destitution and corrupt systems to name a few—Haitians seem to identify more with voodoo than anything else.

Photographer Lynne Warberg, who documented Haitian voodoo for many years, said there's a common saying amongst Haitians:

"Haitians are 70 percent Catholic, 30 percent Protestant, and 100 percent voodoo."

Despite being a recognized religion in Haiti, voodoo lacks a sacred text, organized church or leadership structure. This makes it difficult to define Haitian voodoo. Amongst practitioners, it's considered "a way of life."

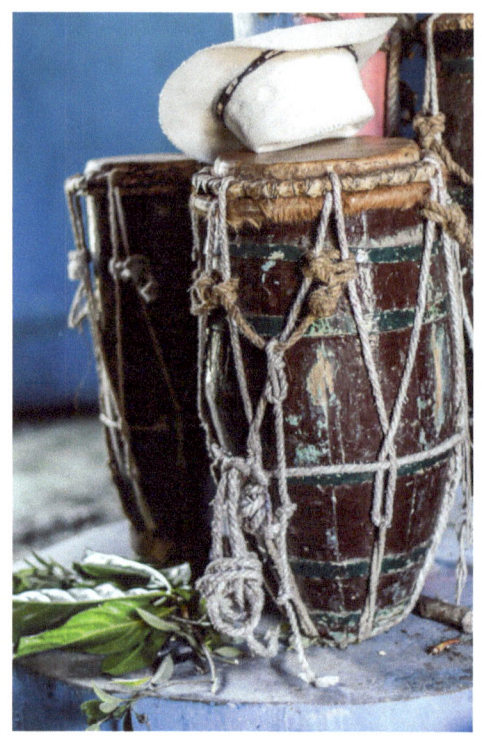
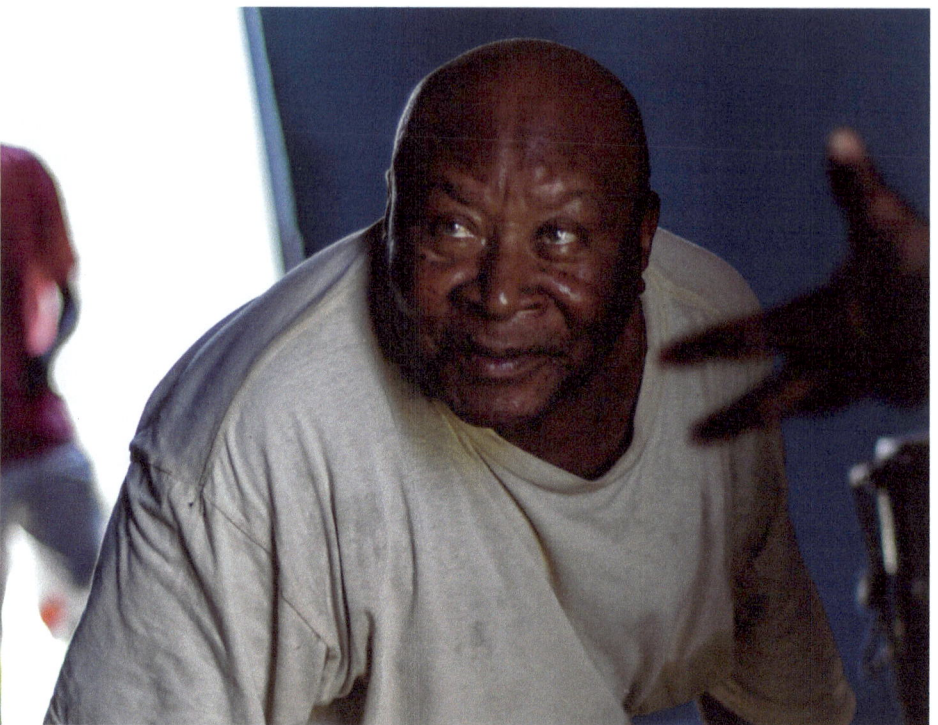

Photos // Johnathan Burkhardt

Voodoo, meaning 'spirit' is considered one of humanity's most ancient traditions, with some scholars estimating that its West African roots go back thousands of years. And it's not just a set of practices—it's an entire worldview.

"Voodoo is a way of life. It's a way of living," explained 46-year-old Johnny Fiefie, who was born in Port-au-Prince, Haiti's capital.

Voodoo determines everything from how to raise one's child to academic views and political awareness, said anthropologist Wade Davis.

Believers gather at voodoo ceremonies to contact spirits, or *Loa* as they are called. The spirits each have a different function, similar to the Greek gods, and some are deified ancestral spirits.

Animals are ceremoniously sacrificed to 'feed' the spirits—in other words, transferring the animal's life energy to the Loa. Each spirit also has a distinct identity, with some being kind and others being fickle or malicious.

While the *Loa* are said to offer the people guidance by communicating through a possessed person or the local priest or priestess, they are also said to express their discontent by punishing the people with sickness.

A Rebel Religion

When thousands of West African slaves were brought to Haiti and forcibly baptized into the Roman Catholic faith, they desperately clung to their African beliefs. But the French colonists viewed voodoo as a threat to their power. So, in an attempt to crush the voodoo practice, they expressly forbid it—and those who disobeyed were whipped, imprisoned or killed. Despite the obvious dangers, slaves continued practicing voodoo secretly while attending Roman Catholic mass weekly. The colonists were fooled. They thought they had successfully converted their West African slaves to Catholicism—but voodoo prevailed.

But why did voodoo remain so central to the slaves' identities?

"Voodoo was indeed one of the few areas of totally autonomous activity for the African slaves," said Carolyn Fick, a Canada Research Fellow at Concordia University in Montreal. "Voodoo ... enabled the slaves to break away psychologically from the very real and concrete chains of slavery and see themselves as independent beings; in short, it gave them a sense of human dignity and enabled them to survive."

If the slaves had not retained their traditions and been unified by voodoo, their fate could have been drastically different. Now, publicly believing in voodoo is significantly less dangerous for practitioners.

Leandre Abellard*

From the outside, it appears to be a normal house—vibrantly painted in the midst of rows of other homes. One wouldn't know by appearances that it's the home of the local voodoo priest.

Leandre Abellard was born into a voodoo legacy. With both parents deeply involved with voodoo, Abellard was trained up in the religion's way. And now, maintaining his priestly connection with the spirits is a method of both self-protection and financial security.

The house consists of one large room with a smaller room connected to it. The main room is mostly empty, except for a pole positioned in the middle alongside ceremonial drums, a variety of leaves and a machete. The walls are coated in vivid blue paint and the ceiling is adorned with paper streamers, also vibrantly colored. There are numerous bystanders observing the situation from chairs and a small cot resting on the dark, dirt floor.

The smaller room off to the left is where Abellard goes to summon the spirits. It's cramped—with room for only a few. A table in that room is covered in food offerings, wine and a bag holding musical shakers for the ceremony. Along the walls are icons of Catholic saints, all representing different Haitian spirits.

When our team of student journalists visited Abellard at his temple in Léogán, the elderly priest greeted them from his place at the center of the room with a smile, his unusual, bright blue eyes having a spellbinding effect. Despite the colorful decorations and the friendly welcome, the energy in the room felt heavy.

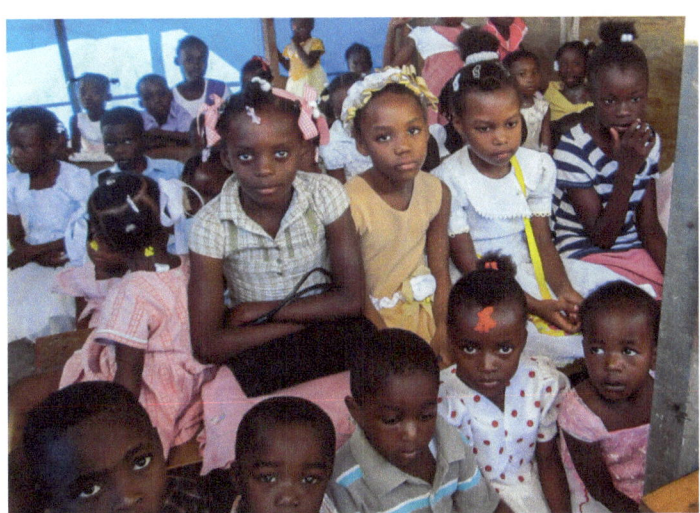

Photo // Harold Rene

* Name has been changed for protection of individual.

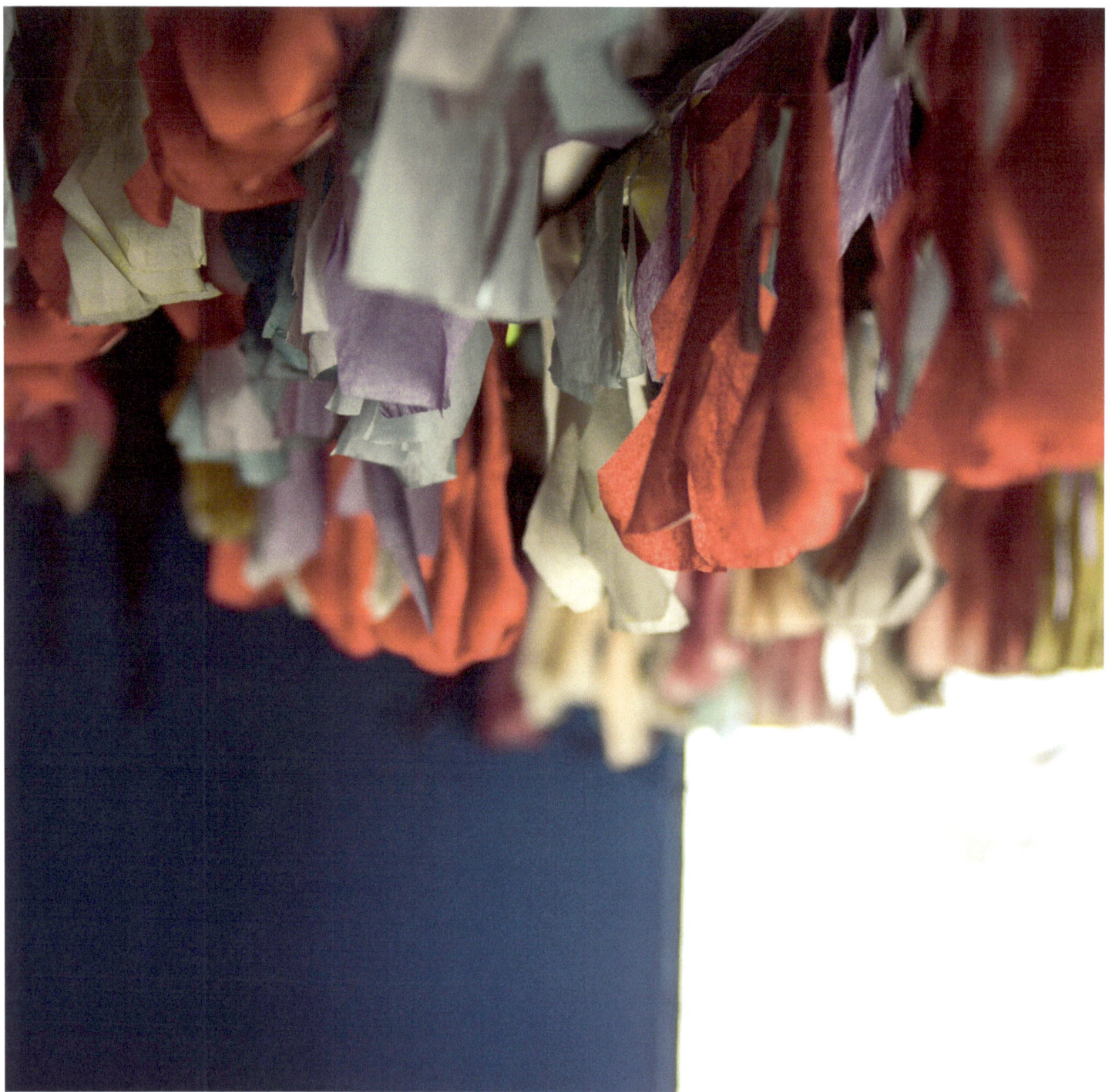

"I knew I was safe, but it felt wrong of me to be there," said Chelsea Wiersma, one of the student journalists on assignment.

Abellard told the team that people from surrounding villages—sometimes even other countries—come to him with needs: wealth, employment, and healing, to name a few. Depending on the needs, he calls certain spirits who are able to meet them—for a price, usually cash. He makes music with ritual instruments, dances and offers the spirits different foods in the hopes that they'll give the people what they came for.

When Wiersma asked Abellard* to describe his ceremonies further, he led her into the smaller side room with the food offerings.

"I'll show you."

Initially, it appeared to be a simple demonstration—but once he began using the shakers to make music and started chanting unintelligibly, it became clear that he was actually summoning the spirits.

"Okay, thank you...," she said as she began to make her way outside.

As she turned to leave, he grabbed her arm and stared directly into her eyes—still chanting steadily.

Jean-Marc, a local Haitian acting as the team's interpreter and guide, shuffled about and laughed nervously before ending the ritual and guiding Wiersma outside.

It meant something that Jean-Marc stopped the ritual, as he already knew Abellard well and had an established relationship with him. His apparent nervousness revealed that the team had become involved in something they had not intended to—something they should walk away from

immediately. Jean-Marc grew up knowing the local priest and says Abellard claims to believe in Jesus—and even goes so far as calling Jesus from the same room he summons the spirits in. According to Jean-Marc, while Abellard has said he will eventually know Christ and convert fully, he knows that his voodoo practice is his livelihood and that he can't abandon it for Christianity at the moment.

As one can see, voodoo is still very much alive in Haiti. It is a complex spiritual worldview that would take a lifetime to comprehend—one that we have just barely begun to learn about. For now, it is enough to get a brief glimpse through the eyes of some of its own.

Neite Decimus

Neite Decimus, a high voodoo priest from Haiti, integrates voodoo with his counseling practice in Massachusetts. He left Haiti in 1997 to study at Bridgewater State University in Massachusetts—and now has a Master's degree in mental health counseling and speaks fluent Haitian Creole, English, Spanish and French.

Voodoo is a tradition in Decimus' family, as his great-grandfather, grandfather and father were all high priests in Port-au-Prince, Haiti's capital. While Decimus watched his father use herbal potions to heal people, he didn't want to follow in the footsteps of the generations before him. He wanted to study law. Shortly after, he experienced what seemed to be a series of prophetic dreams. Initially, Decimus assumed they were coincidence, until his deceased grandfather appeared in one and told him to follow his destiny—that destiny, Decimus realized, was to become a high priest of voodoo.

He immersed himself in the study of voodoo. Now, people come to see him for everything from physical pain to personal problems—and he uses his voodoo expertise and tradition to assist them within the context of his counseling

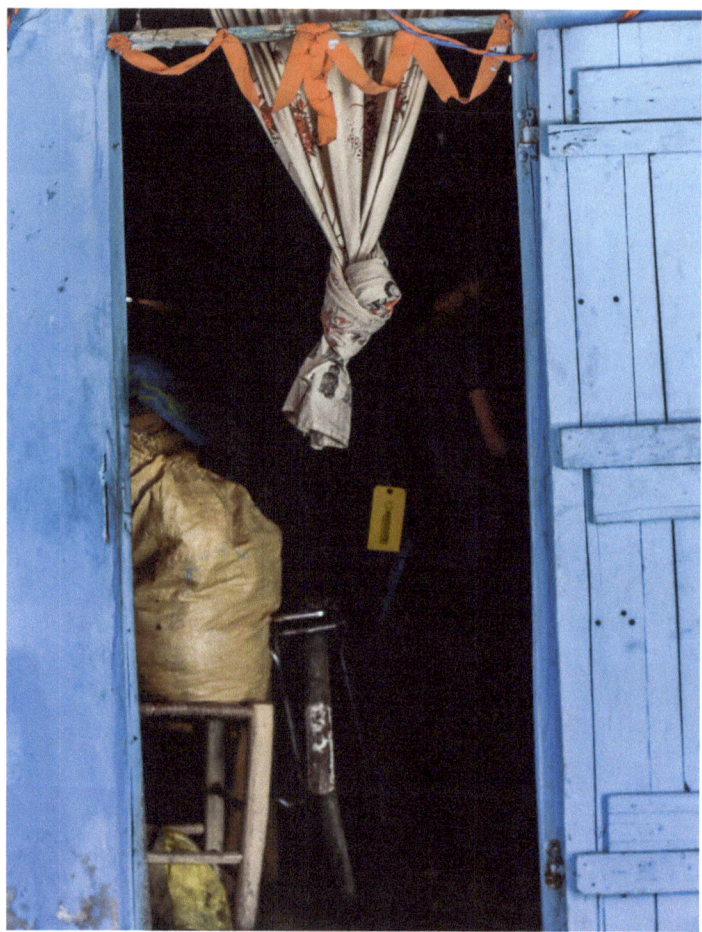

Photo // Johnathan Burkhardt

sessions. We had the opportunity to speak with him over the phone about his experiences with voodoo and his homeland of Haiti.

How is voodoo connected to physical healing?

Neite Decimus: "If you have a headache ... [people] always say 'take some Tylenol.' But it's not that ... you might have a problem in your tooth or eye to create the headache. In voodoo, what we do ... [we] seek the problem your body has through the energy to heal you ... we measure your energy."

So many researchers have misunderstood the connection between voodoo and Catholicism. Could you give your take?

Neite Decimus: "The freedom I have today my dad [also a voodoo priest] did not have. My dad had to be forced to say he was a Catholic ... he was lying to himself. Nobody can make me say I am a Catholic. You will see a lot of people from my country—they will try to marry another person and lie [about their worldview] to become legal. If we want to follow the rules, we need to help understand the rules of the game [by pretending to be Catholic]. Catholics and Protestants are fighting voodoo. The Catholics think they're better because they come from civilization. No civilization is better than others. Materials don't make you superior ... I am not saying they are not good. If a person wants to help me, [they] do not need to tell me not to do voodoo anymore. I will not use it to kill, no! We need to learn to respect one another."

Many think that voodoo is about pin-stuck voodoo dolls and black magic. What do you think are the biggest misconceptions about voodoo?

Neite Decimus: "Nobody takes time to learn about [voodoo]. Not too many people have the chance to talk about it with people like me. And when you have this knowledge ... it's power. Remember when the earthquake happened? Some people said it's because we believe in voodoo. And the Cholera ... some said the source of the Cholera was voodoo. Last week a person had an accident and three voodoo priests were killed ... but no one talked about that because there [had been] an auto accident and they claimed that the voodoo priests created that accident. Everything that happens, they blame it on voodoo because they don't want the teachings. They think we are servants of Satan. We need to work hand to hand to make life better ... when [we] sit down to share ideas about why we are here, we will make a better world. That's what voodoo teaches people."

What do you think Haiti needs right now?

Neite Decimus: "To teach people things ... if you have kids and never send them to school, how do you think they will compete in this highly educated world? We need to be the voice of the voiceless, the eyes of the blind and the ears of the deaf—so we can create a society where everybody feels that when they cry out, people listen to them. Now, anything a person can [do to] help Haiti is help us have schools around the country. I will feel great if all Haitians can go to school as they do here in the U.S. We want to create a society where everyone will have their fair share."

What are your feelings towards those who may be trying to help? Including NGOs.

Neite Decimus: "We have more hypocrites who come to Haiti to help ... most of them are NGOS. Giving someone a loaf of bread every day won't help them ... You teach them how to bake their own bread. And some people bring guns to Haiti. We don't need guns ... we need to grow the animals, to create food—why do people have guns? Those are the hypocrites."

What is the best way to rebuild Haiti?

Neite Decimus: "It's not how many houses you have. Rebuilding a country is to bring people to [the] knowledge that they know they're worth something. Through their being, they will create. It's organizations ... they create schools. They taught people discipline. We need to help the new generation to understand who they are, where they come from and who they are as people. If we are as history told us—the son and daughter of slaves—and the slaves were working for other people for hundreds of years, where is the profit of the money they were working for? We do not have any materials, but we still have human beings."

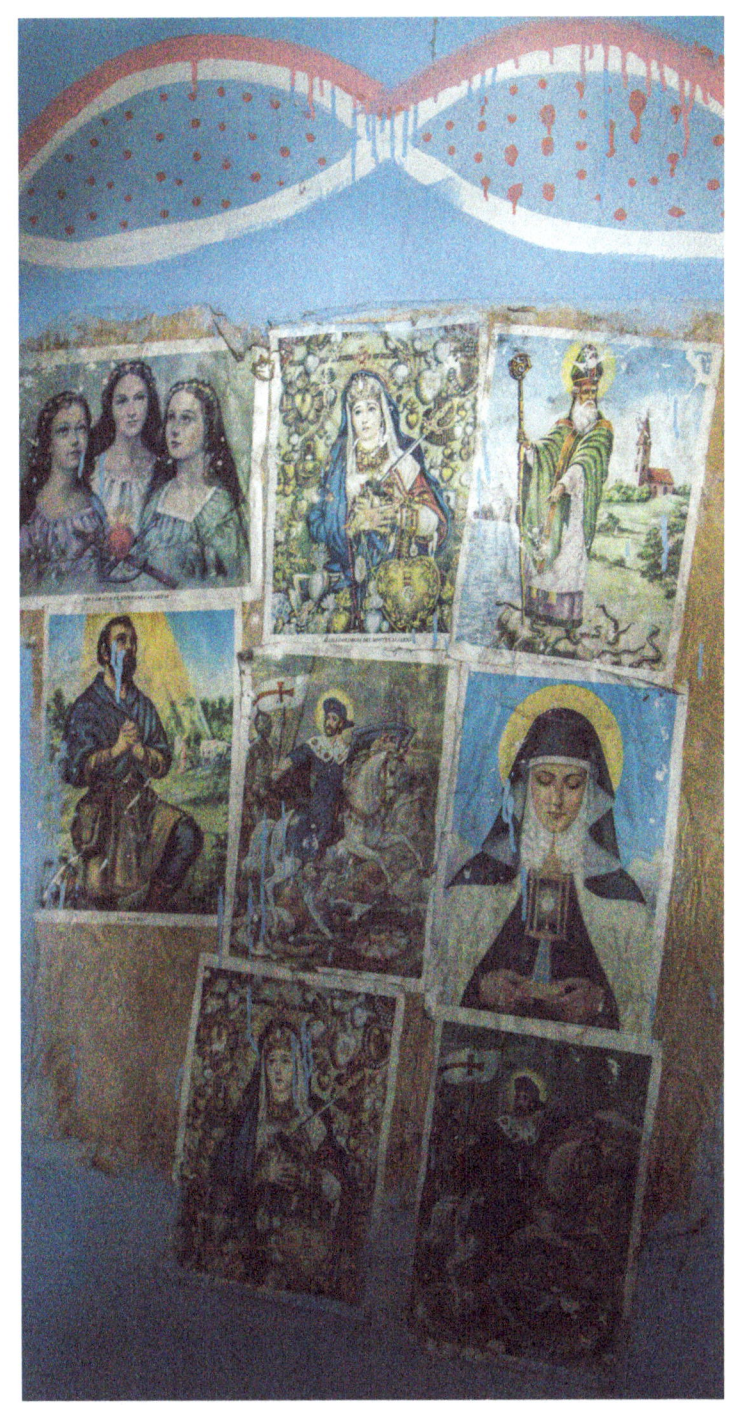

Photo // Shayna Broadsky

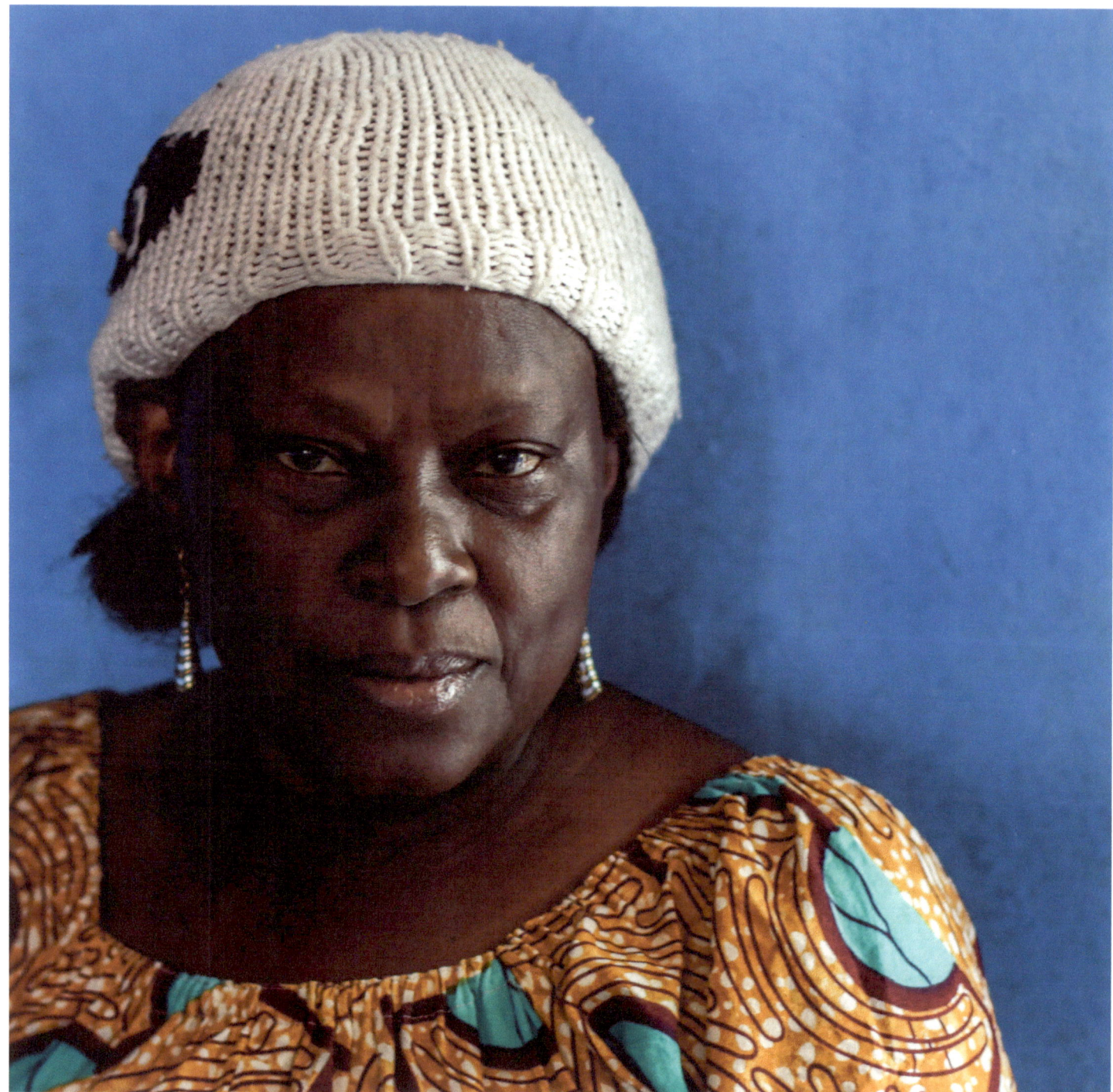

Chapter 3
Christianity and Catholicism

"If we have opportunity to work in a place like this where you meet many people who invest in voodoo, it is the best place to meet many people to invest their hearts in Jesus," said Pastor Yonel Delafranc Regis, who has been a pastor in Port-au-Prince for 23 years.

He has taught in many different churches all over Haiti, facing much spiritual warfare and tribulation. He explained that even if the situation looks difficult, it is good in God's eyes because as it says in the Bible, God is not coming for the healthy people, but for the unhealthy. Pastor Regis considers those who practice voodoo 'the unhealthy.'

Although voodoo and spirituality are prevalent all through-out Haiti, many Christians view this as a means of opening conversations about Christ.

Regis explains that he does not find his strength in himself or his own words, but in the Lord.

"The people who plant water are nothing, but the Lord who allowed the plant to grow is everything," Regis said.

Ask any Haitian, and they will tell you that spiritual warfare is prevalent in Haiti. Regis explained this by describing how "in some services of prayer in his church, you feel the Holy Ghost visit you and assist you. The power of the Holy Spirit touches the people."

Everyone in Haiti recognizes the power of voodoo and "bad" spirits in Haiti. However, Christians in the country say that the power that they have is much stronger. This is where they find their hope.

"When you have Christ, it's like you have a shield around you," explained Jerry Joseph, a 27-year-old Haitian man who has lived in Port-au-Prince his entire life.

Regis also explained that many people in Haiti feel that "the power of bad spirits mistreats them," meaning that spiritual warfare is present everywhere. Haitians feel that they are in the midst of a constant fight spiritually.
"This creates fights between the power of God and the power of demons," he said.

Although some Haitians such as Pastor Regis and Jerry are living in Christ, the demons may still be able to grab onto them.

"Poverty is so hard in Haiti, even if they have hope in Christ, sometimes within the fight in their life between the hope of Christ and the poverty," he said. He went on to explain that the poverty will retain them and hold them back from following Christ because of fear of losing even more.

The demons will ask them, "Why are you poor then and hungry? Why does your God not give you what you need?"

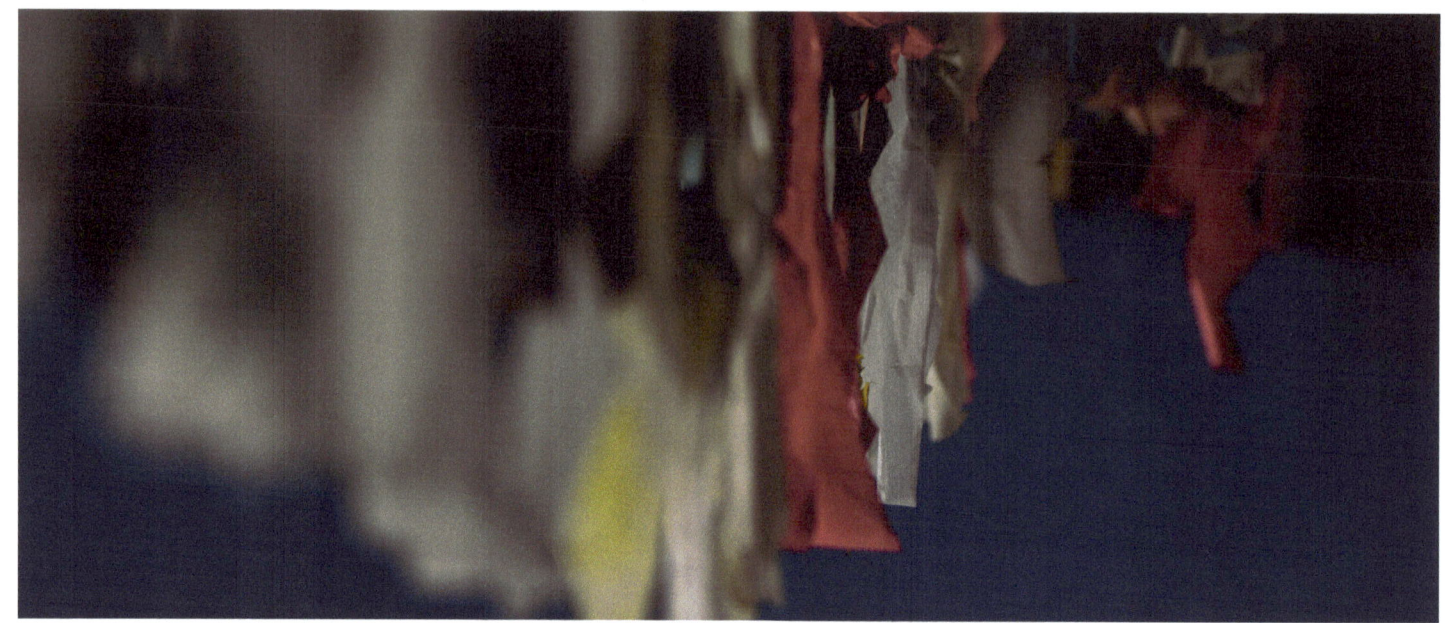

This makes it very tempting to give in to the voices that accuse.

"Satan and demons can give you money but you will pay the consequence. One day Satan will randomly kill your child," explained Regis. He says that seeking Jesus is the only sure way to resist. He said that you need to return quickly to Jesus.

Despite this fear that Pastor Regis spoke of, most Christian Haitians do not fear the evil spirits. They know that the God they serve is more powerful and can protect them. Joseph Walner is a Christian Haitian, living in Leogane, Haiti. He said that he serves Jesus, who has all the power. He knows that the promises Jesus has made will be kept wherever he is. Whenever in the presence of evil spirits, Walner said that he just prays inside of him.

"I prayed to God to forbid his spirit to come. The spirit of God was inside us. With his spirit, which is inside us, nothing bad can hurt us," he said. "The spirit is our protection. What the spirit of God doesn't want to enter inside of us, it won't be able to enter because he is our protection."

It may seem very difficult to remain a Christian in a place where nearly all of your neighbors are worshipping different spirits and partaking in different religious practices. Many Haitians that believe in the Catholic faith will integrate voodoo and Catholic elements. The majority of Haitians, regardless if they are Protestant Christian or not, do believe in the evil spirits. 80 percent of Haitians are Roman Catholic, 16 percent are Protestant Christian, and 4 percent are non-religious. However, according to a New York Times article written in 2010, nearly 95 percent of all Haitians practice at least certain elements of voodoo, often in conjunction with Catholicism. With that being said, this is how one knows that their faith is so strong. Everything around them is convincing them that voodoo may be the answer. But even so, they do not stop fighting and believing.

One of the biggest turning points for religion in Haiti was the earthquake of 2010. When the earthquake took place, many Haitians took to the streets. They joined together in worship and praise.

"There was singing and crying out to God all night," said Jerry Joseph, a 28-year-old Haitian that was living in Port-au-Prince at the time of the earthquake. After the earthquake, people flocked to religious influences, both Christian and voodoo alike. They sang hymns, attended religious services and listened to the missionaries and aid workers.

"Religion is at the heart of Haitian society...the earthquake has led to an increase reference to religion and to churches," explained Yolette Etienne, the Haiti Program Director for Oxfam in Mole St. Nicholas.

Many were criticized for their belief in voodoo and voodoo was blamed for being the reason for all of the natural disasters. Others believed that God permitted the earthquake. Also, many Christian organizations responded to the earthquake with aid and support.

"For a religion that's supposedly the national religion for the Haitian people [voodoo], it's amazingly absent in the earthquake phenomena," said Gerald Murray, a University of Florida anthropologist who carried out extensive fieldwork in Haiti.

Haiti has many needs—political, economic and environmental, to name a few. But according to many Haitians, as far as hope goes, spiritual needs are the first that need to be met. This gives many Haitians a love for the people in their country and a hope for the future.

"Spiritual problem is in seeing the real God. Solve that first and then you can solve the others. Haiti for Christ and Christ for Haiti," said Regis.

He always remembers 2 Chronicles 7:14 which reads, "If my people who are called by my name humble themselves, and pray and seek my face and turn from their wicked ways, then I will hear from heaven and will forgive their sin and heal their land."

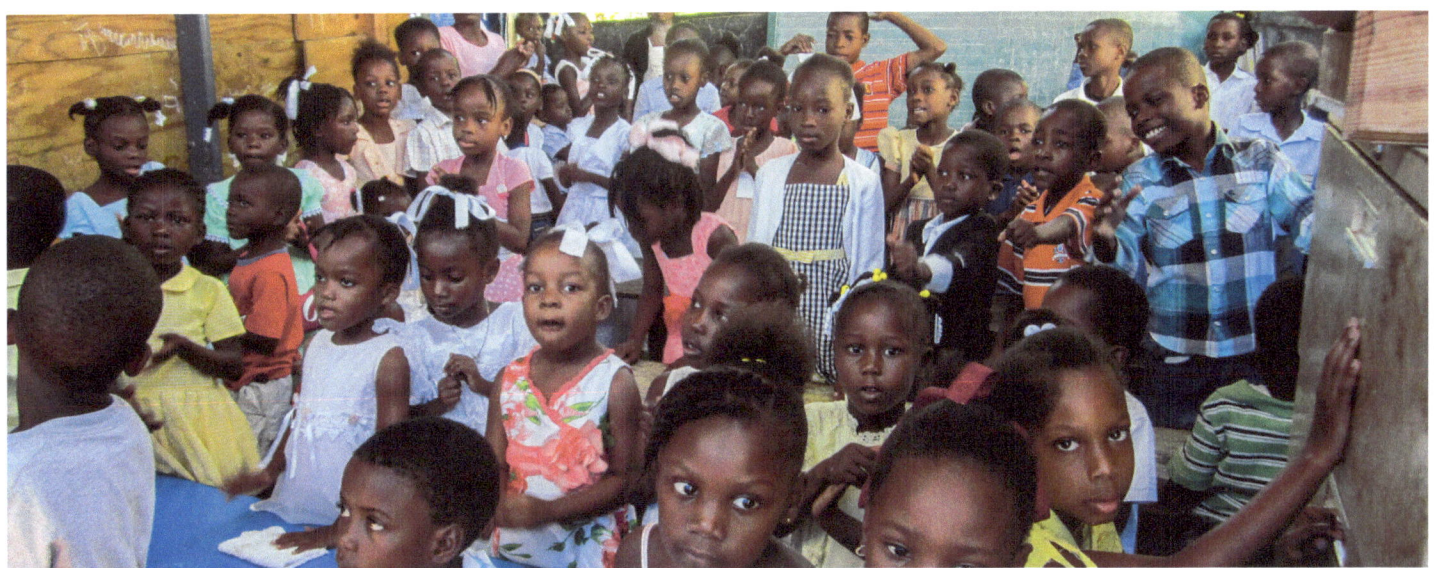

Photo // Harold Rene

Receiving Hands

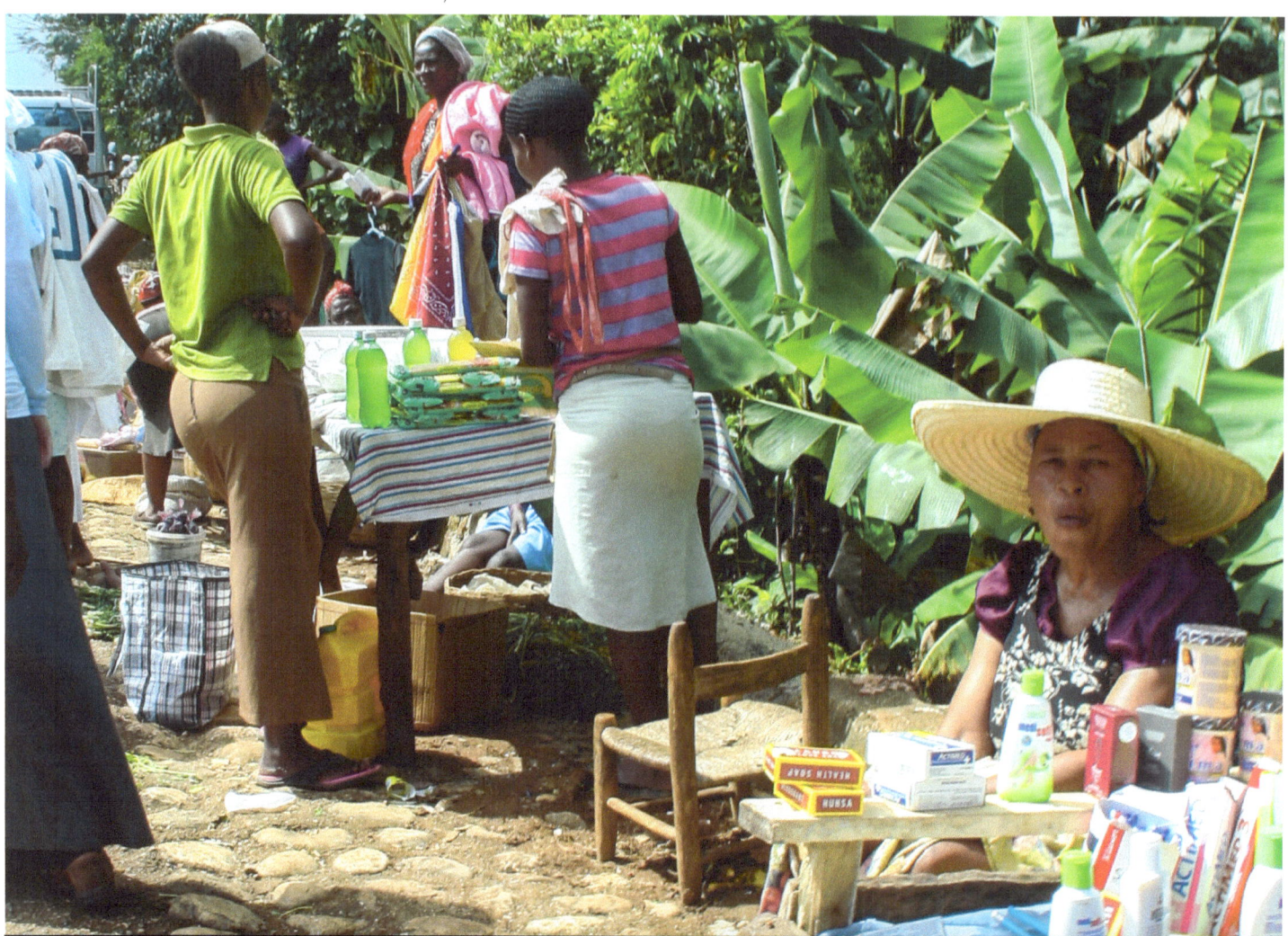

"The more they're born and can't attend school, the more percentage of uneducated people adds—whom because of not having a profession, lack of job and knowledge and wanting to survive—will cause an insecurity problem in the country, causing many of our Haitians and other people who could be helpful in participating in Haiti's development leave, and are afraid to come back."

- Larson

Photo // Delopherne Fabrice

Chapter 4
Haitians and the Government

"A job, a school, food and security are what people claim for, so if someone can come up with some nice words giving hope to the highest percentage of people in needy...You will have as many votes that you wish..." said Larsen, a teenage translator from Port-au-Prince.

Five years after the earthquake in Haiti, protests over gas prices and simultaneous demands for the resignation of President Martelly dominated the streets of Port-au-Prince and the media's narrative.

It's easy to see an American perspective in the chaos. On the surface, everyday Haitians are only demanding the life, liberty and pursuit of happiness taken for granted by their northern neighbors.

But an American similarity doesn't imply an Americanized solution. Because when Haitians demand lower gas prices, they do it for food, shelter, the ability to see family members far away. This is not a demand for cheaper road trips and or a more cost-effective standard of living.

This is a demand for a standard in the first place.

In February 2015, only a month from the quake's anniversary, falling gas prices were in the news in every country, and though the dip would soon be ubiquitous in America, Haitians found their country's exclusion from the phenomenon to be yet another fault to add to the long list of grievances against their leaders.

Minibus driver Loédon Gaspard told the Daily Mail that if gasoline prices were falling worldwide, it should be the same in Haiti.

"We are poor; we cannot live anymore," said Gaspard.

Prime Minister Evans Paul tried to quell protesters by insisting that the government cannot lower the gas prices.

"It's not that we do not want to; it's because we are not able to," Paul said.

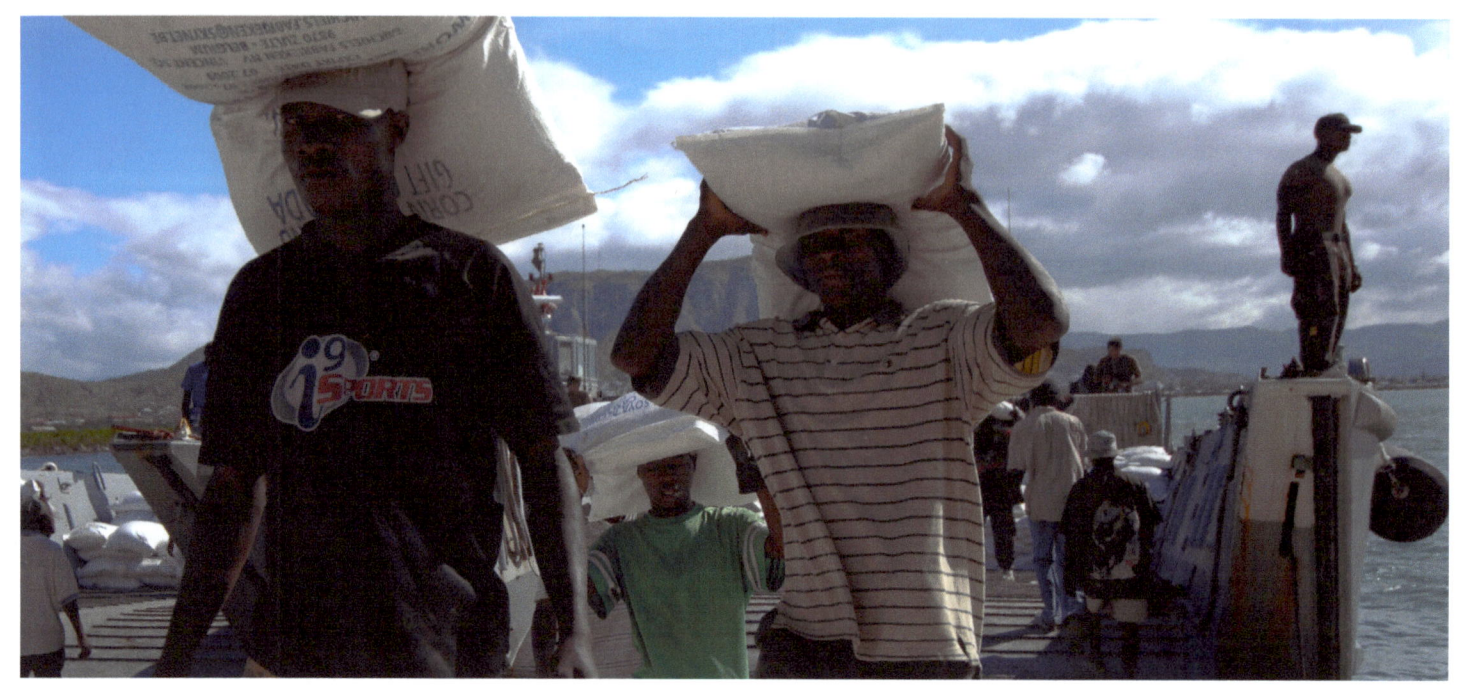

But the people remembered their small victory, when similar protests forced shadowy powers to lower prices by a precious 20 cents.

"Remember you were one of us from the ghetto."

When France24 news cameras panned the protesters blocking streets with burning car tires, men would step up to the lens with a message for their leaders.

"Prime Minister Evans Paul, remember you were one of us from the ghetto. And without us, you wouldn't be where you are today," said one man, with determined eyes and a voice brimming with bitterness.

He continued:

"President Martelly, without the people, you wouldn't be president today. Remember all the promises you made to us?"

"You have lied to us."

NGO's picking up the pieces

While politicians struggle for the positions at the top, a power vacuum widens in the rest of Haiti. Local government has collapsed, and with it, sound economic structures and enforcers of order.

NGO's have stepped in, for better or for worse.

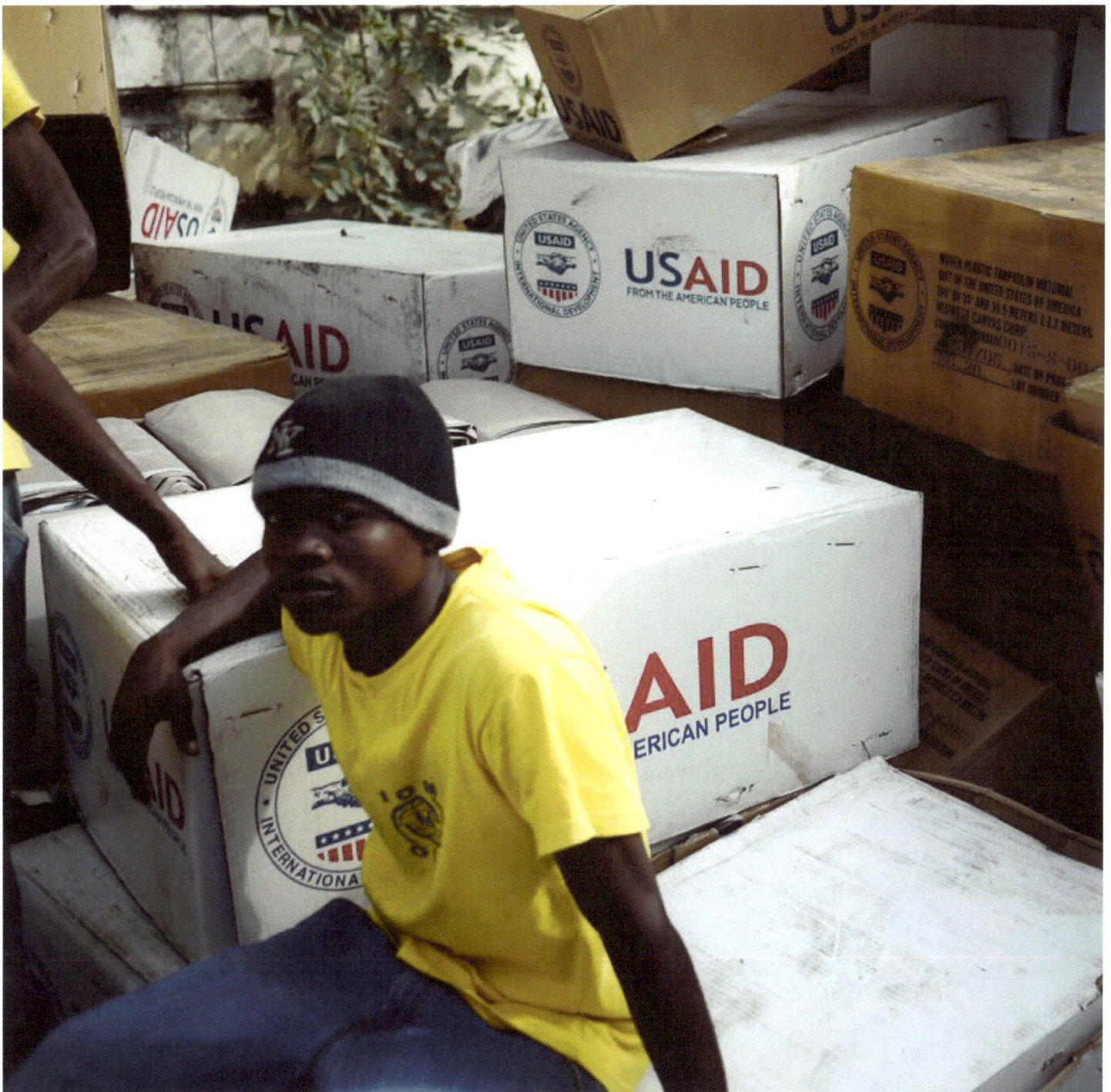

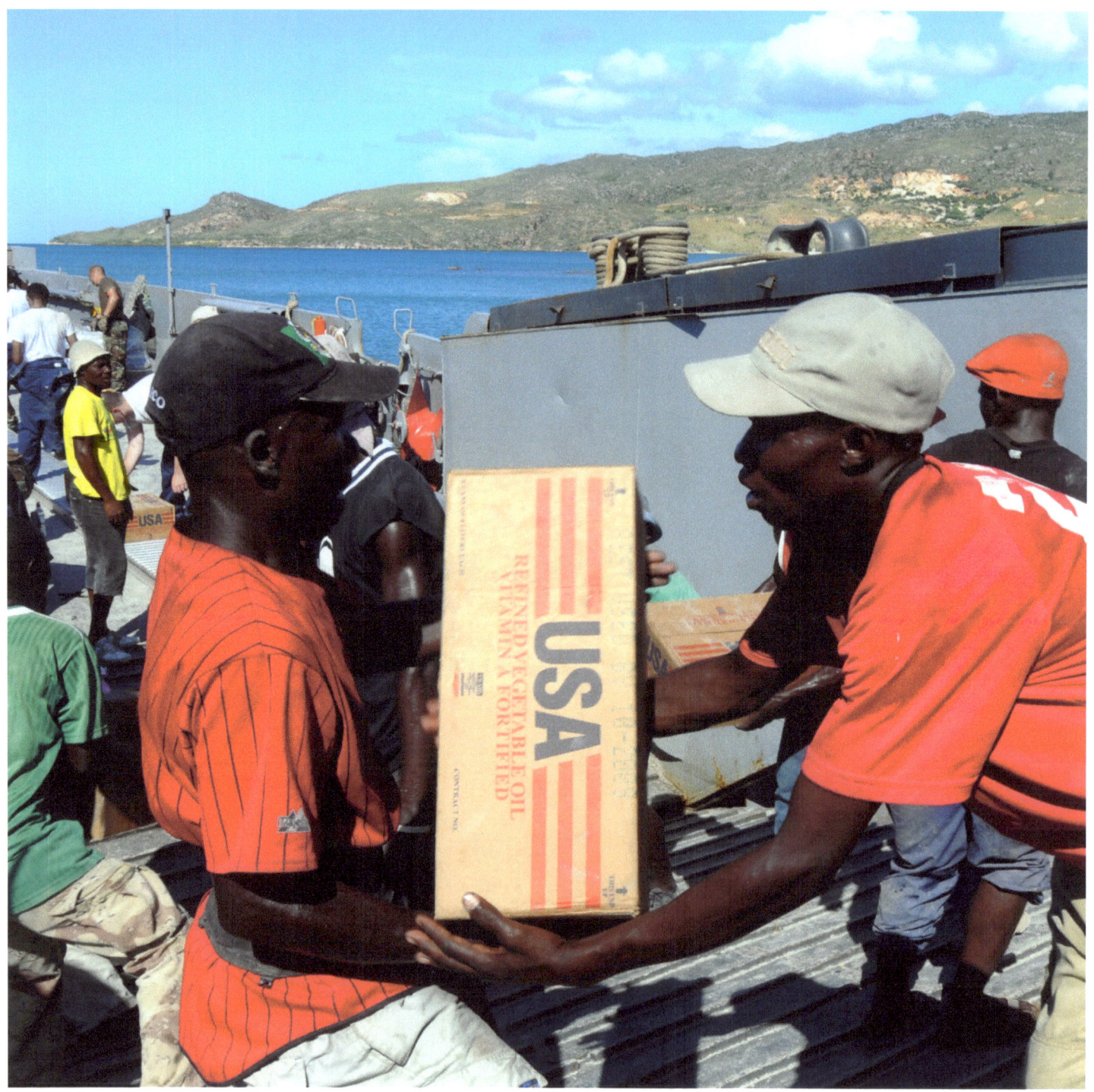

Chapter 5
Non-Government Organizations

We followed the tattoo artist/pastor from the repurposed tavern into his parlor after singing Drinking Psalms from handmade hymnals. Corrigan Clay sat down in the swivel chair behind a glass table where he keeps his paperwork, cash register and small model of a "Cliche Tat Man." Behind him a sign reads "tipping makes it hurt less." He looked somber. He had just preached a difficult Easter sermon on the sacrifice of love and the pain of death. The service was small, about fifteen people, a few of them children. The stocky tattooed pastor played the part of both the pastor and the worship leader, singing his heart out through his Irish goatee.

When asked about NGO's, a point of contention and the topic of much heated debate, he smiles pleasantly and begins to pour out his knowledge on the topic in such a casual fashion it seems as though he had kicked up his feet on his coffee table at home and leaned back into his favorite La-Z-Boy chair. Corrigan wraps NGO's into a neat little package as organizations that "do any kind of charitable service."

Anyone seeking a formal definition will find one on a page at NGO.org, a very unimaginative United Nations website. The official definition is as follows:

> A non-governmental organization (NGO) is any non-profit, voluntary citizens' group which is organized on a local, national or international level. Task-oriented and driven by people with a common interest, NGOs perform a variety of service and humanitarian functions, bring citizen concerns to Governments, advocate and monitor policies and encourage political participation through provision of information.

> Some are organized around specific issues, such as human rights, environment or health. They provide analysis and expertise, serve as early warning mechanisms and help monitor and implement international agreements. Their relationship with offices and agencies of the United Nations system differs depending on their goals, their venue and the mandate of a particular institution.

Formal definitions aside, when people talk about NGOs, they classify them in two groups: those that provide relief and those that provide development.

Relief work is reactionary. It's emergency work done when disaster strikes—like the 7.0 earthquake that struck Haiti on January 12, 2010. The quick slip between the Caribbean and North American tectonic plates sent out waves of energy that leveled much of the city, did major damage to the limited sewage and clean water systems, and overwhelmed the already inadequate medical care available in the country. Relief agencies rushed in and provided shelter, food, water, clothes and medical support. Without the help of organizations like the American Red Cross, Food For The Poor and Compassion International, the already massive loss of life would have been far more severe. However relief work can only last for so long.

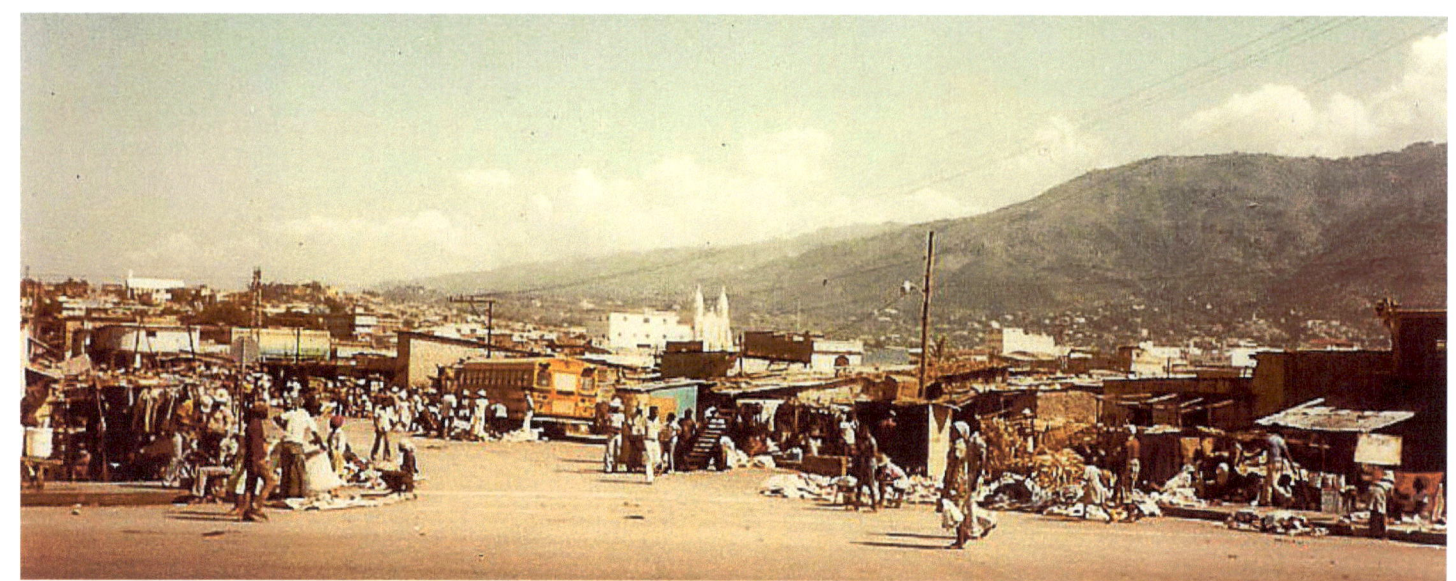

Those who go into a country to help want to eventually leave, or at least not be needed any longer. That is where development organizations come in to play. A country needs to be able to support itself. Third world countries affected by natural disasters need more than just food and shelter; they need to be prepared to handle an event like it in the future.

New Missions, an NGO started in 1983, now has 22 churches and 22 schools in Haiti where they are educating Haitians to equip and empower them to make their country a better place. The concept is the same as the classic proverb, "Give a man a fish and you feed him for a day; teach a man to fish and you feed him for a lifetime." The idea is that when the NGO's all leave the country, they won't have to come back because the Haitians will be equipped to solve the problems in their own creative ways.

The trouble is that there seems to be no end to the NGO occupation of Haiti. NGO's existed in Haiti decades before the earthquake, so many Haitians fear that they will remain for decades to come. After the earthquake there was a large influx of NGO's dogpiling the already suffocating infrastructure of Haiti. There might have been some space to breathe if the work had been quick, but 5 years later relief work is still being done. Those concerned that relief work will only stop when the people are able to care for themselves have made a push for more development work to be done. It is true, there is much development to be done. Opinions are flung all around and theories of how to really fix Haiti abound.

Craig Erickson, a 25 year old student at Biola University, alongside a fellow student named Brendon Anthony, age 22, started Harvestcraft as a way of helping Haitian farmers grow crops in sustainable ways. The organization utilizes urban and agricultural designs to grow a variety of crops. As an NGO operator in Haiti, he has seen first-hand the problems of well intentioned helpers all arriving in one place at the same time.

He observed, "Everyone knows that what they are doing is what they are supposed to be doing and that their way is the best way."

Haiti is a petri dish and a battleground. NGO's from all over are trying to fix the country in the way they think best. The problem is that none of these benevolent scientists know what the effects of their experiment will be. What's worse is they are all conducting experiments that are disjointed from one another. They are like scientists in battle fatigues, making war with one another to fix the country.

"With the government there is some kind of communication going on, you've got the department of health, the department of education etc," he said.

The problem is that NGO's are serving the people in all of the ways that a government should be. The NGO's feed the people, they educate the people, create new jobs, provide health care and protection, build roads, and establish sanitation systems. The difference is that they lack the unity and oversight a government can provide. The obvious solution is to give all the money and power to the government and everything is better, right? Unfortunately, it isn't that simple.

Haiti's government is a mess, and their political history isn't the cleanest. A country that was born out of a slave revolution, has seen dictators rise and fall, and even a Catholic Priest that declared Voodoo an official religion, has trouble trusting the people in power. Some claim that you have to be corrupt in order to enter government work, and those that are not corrupt are too afraid to step in. Other governments and organizations are suspicious of the government as well. When money is put into the government project as promised, then delayed, at one point or another the money simply disappears. For this reason, the role of surrogate government that the NGO's are playing can be a good thing for Haiti.

Though they are disjointed, they are serving to keep Haitians alive while out of the hands of a corrupt government. What Haiti really needs is a change in heart. Those operating NGO's hope that the Haitian people will learn and be able to develop, to grow into a safer more civilized culture where disease and ignorance are less rampant. In some ways technology and education can help, but when given the sole emphasis we simply make men as C.S.Lewis said, "more clever devils."

The work that truly needs to be done is heart development. Without the development of character, all other work is pointless. All other work can be twisted and abused, helping a culture to survive into the future, but what is a future where people are killing, stealing, and oppressing? Food and water can be hoarded, education can be used to oppress or those educated can leave for better opportunity, and money can be spent on personal desires rather than going to the good of the people. In order to make a full recovery all areas need to be addressed in a unified manner.

When people are being fed and getting their medical needs taken care of there need to be NGO's to equip and educate the people to think into the future so that they can stop relying on others to hand them things. At the same time there need to be programs and churches teaching the spiritual principles of self sacrificial love. The damage that has been done to Haiti has been against the whole human being, their mind, body and soul. Only when all three are addressed at the same time can true healing and restoration come. Haiti's recovery has not, and will not be a speedy one; there may be a generation between now and the new Haiti to come, but young men like Larson show that a new heart is beginning to form, and this heart is full of courage, full of wisdom, and full of hope.

Working Hands

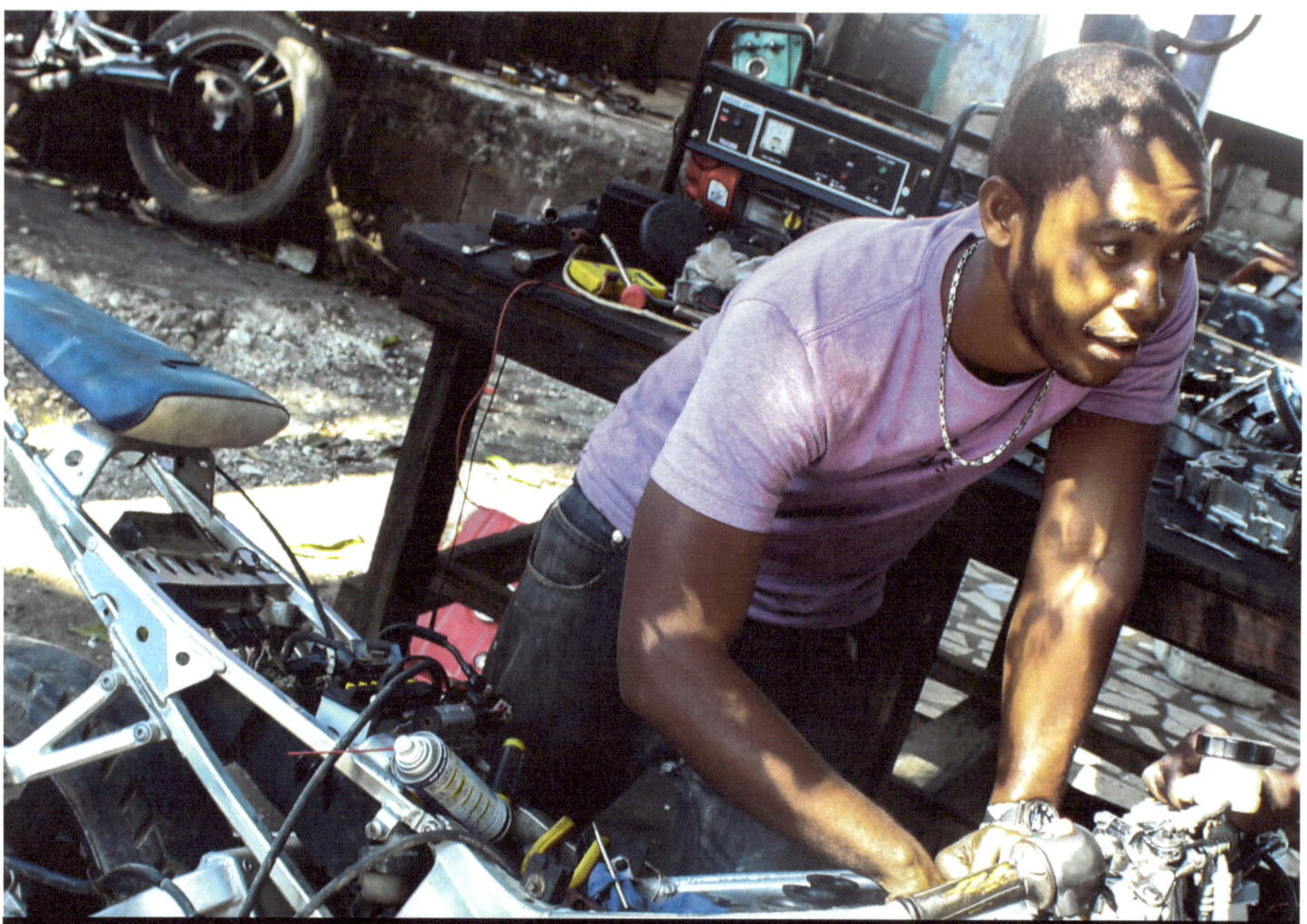

"So many people with a good profession, who've studied enough for many years, can't use or work on their profession, and are taken for lazy people once being seen often home or by the streets, and are forced to believe that it's impossible for any goals achievement in Haiti, and must leave to realize what they've always dreamed of. Family, friends, close people, those who know or have heard about you and have watched you grow up and sometimes even oneself will start counting years left for a success life, what can be achieved and who you can become. there must come a day when no Haitians leave for a better life, but for those out ot come with no fear feeling free to come live in their beautiful country."

- Larson

Photo // Holophene Thierry

Chapter 6
The Economy

Haiti, being the poorest country in the Americas, has relied on outside organizations and other countries for decades. Because of this, many outside organizations are in Haiti working to stabilize the country's economy. With a high rate of poverty, men, women and children go hungry, sometimes for days, even weeks. Hundreds of stories about mud cookies that mothers make for their children come from the streets of the capital Port-au-Prince. There are natural resources in the country, but with low input comes low output. A highly ingrained class system and discrimination stops progress of all citizens trying to make a better life for themselves and their families. All of these obstacles compound onto one another and stifle advances in the Haitian economy.

The Haitian economy is ridden with poverty, malnutrition, class discrimination, deforestation, poor soil conditions that are highly susceptible to erosion, and imbalanced imports and exports. According to the United States Agency for International Development (USAID) around 40 percent of Haitians are unemployed. This unemployment rate affects not only those unemployed, but also their families, friends and support systems. Haitians have many obstacles in the way of employment, which then leads to hunger, malnutrition and even starvation, especially in children.

Why is there so much hunger? Why is there so much need for food? Because of Haiti's terrain, agriculture and farming food crops are not sustainable. Haiti has a more mountainous terrain than Switzerland, which means the acres of cultivable and farmable land are extremely limited. Much of the land is susceptible to erosion. The crops are limited to things such as sugar, coffee, corn and beans. Other factors, such as disease and government-required slaughter, have devastated the livestock of Haiti. Even with around half of the workforce taking jobs in agriculture, about 50 percent of food is imported.

Because of the gross imbalance of the economic structure in Haiti, men and women are working at providing for themselves in different ways. Through farms and gardens, Haitians are working for themselves and their community, providing food and nutrients to many who would otherwise rely on large organizations to provide imported food or receive nothing at all. Trade workers, woodworkers, artists, street vendors, brick masons and metal workers all strive each day to provide for their family. Through hard work and determination, Haitians are overcoming numerous obstacles to pursue an independent life. Here are stories of the broken rebuilding, the devastated finding hope through laboring alongside their countrymen and finding hope in everyday work.

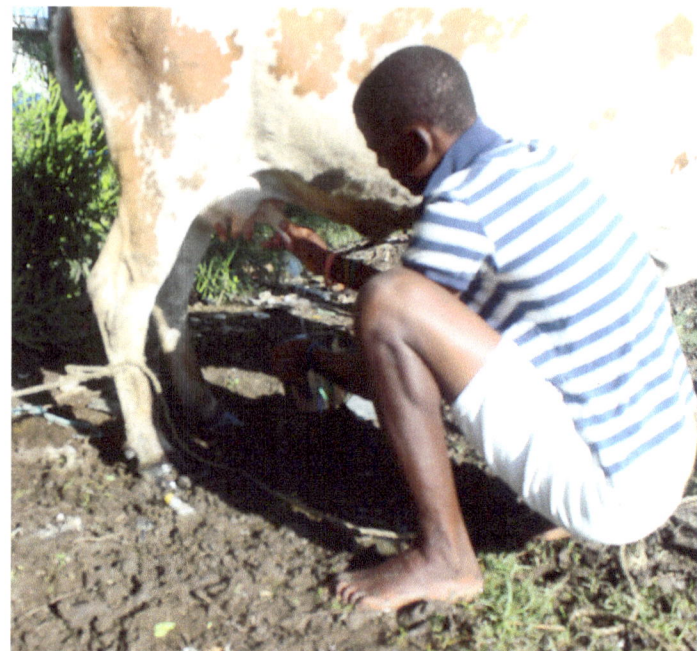

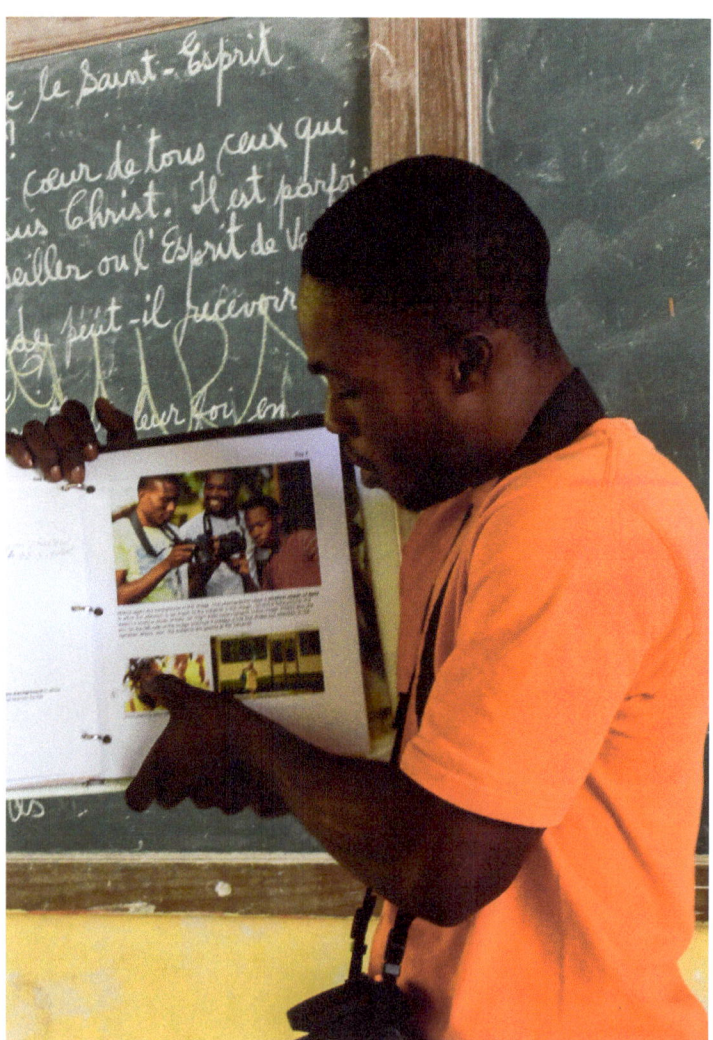

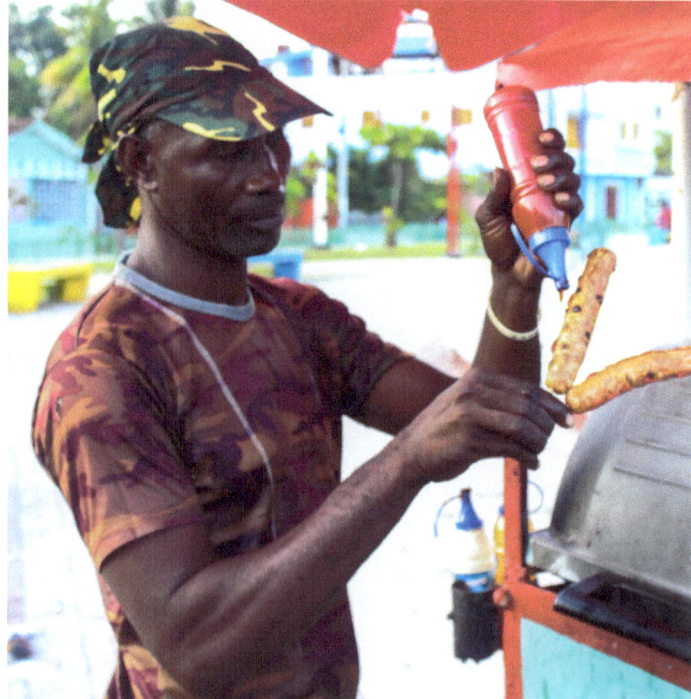

Photos // Joseph Walner (left), Holophene Thierry (top right), Holophene Thierry (bottom right)

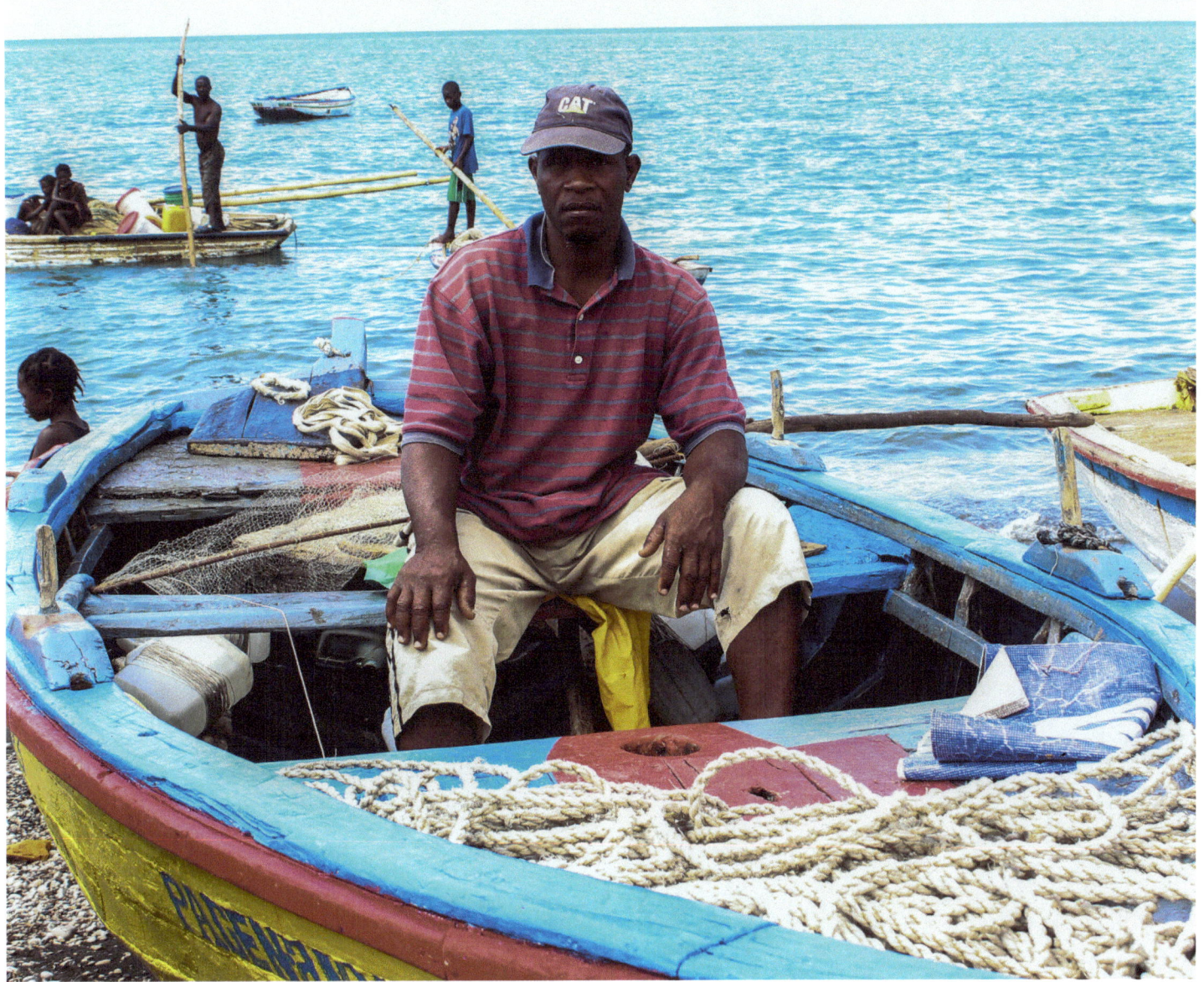

Photo // Jean-Jacques Hosiella

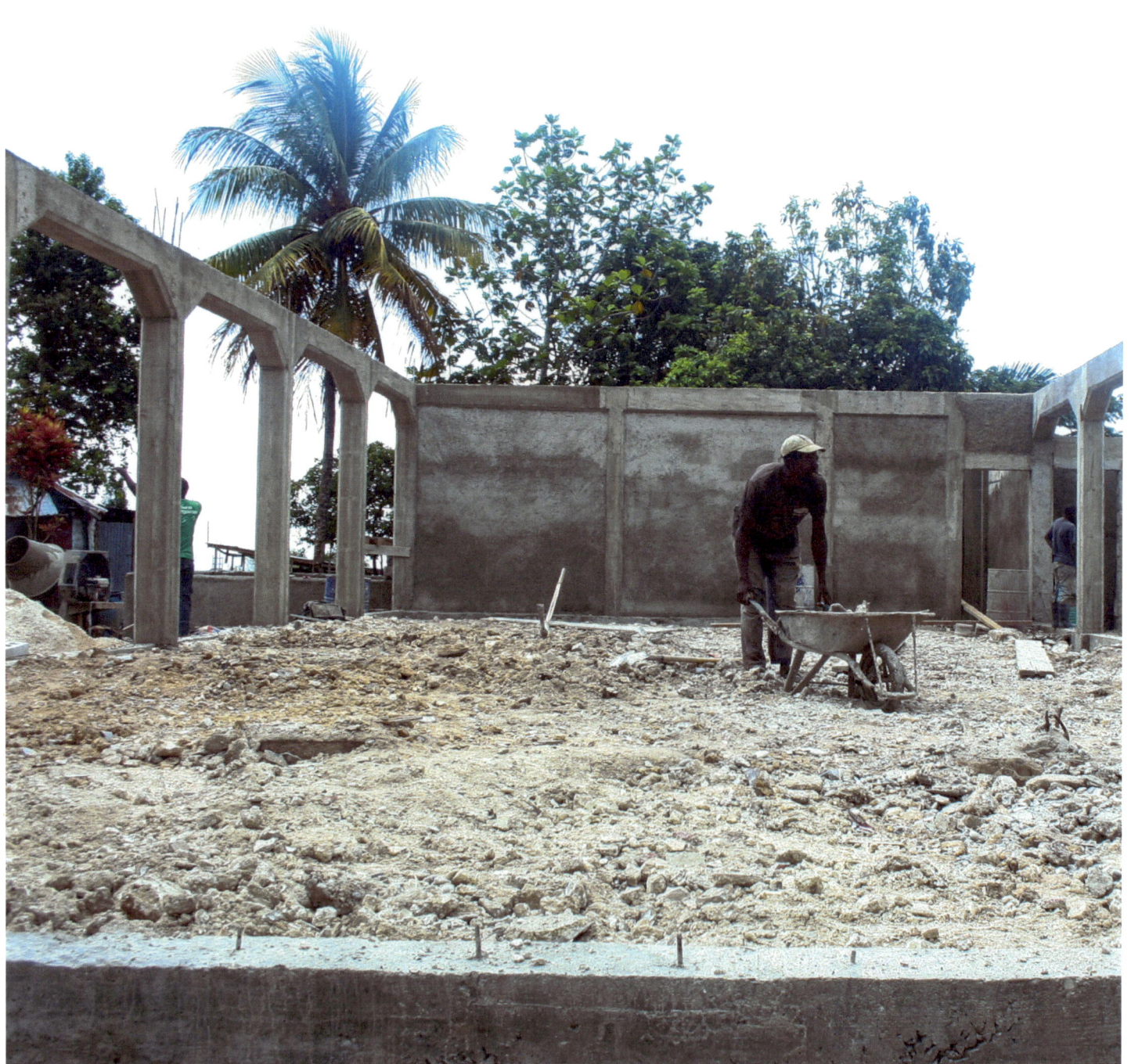

Chapter 7
The Workers

The following are first hand accounts of Haitians describing their own jobs. Details were taken from interviews conducted in Port-au-Prince and in the Leogane region of Haiti during April 2015.

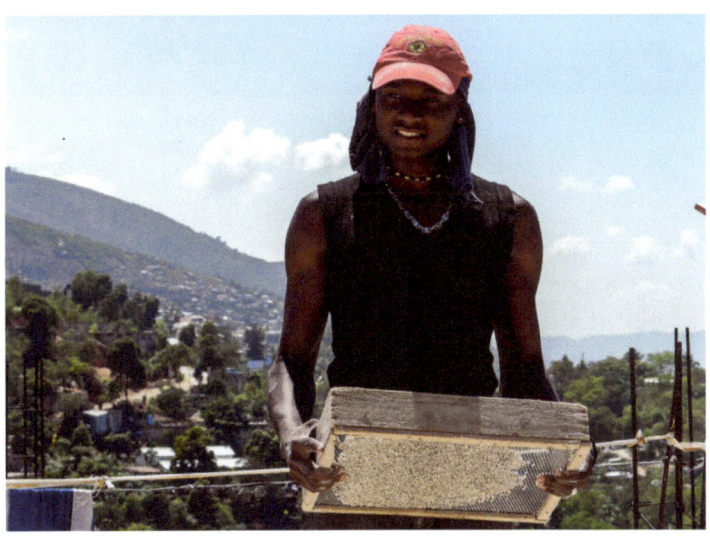

Photo // Johnathan Burkhardt

Brick Maker, Frankey, 25 years old

I started his type of work because of my foreman, he called and told me to start doing construction work. I have been doing [brick making] for 3 years now and I enjoy it. It gets hot in the sun but I am used to the heat now. I support my mother and father with my job. Every Saturday I get paid 70 haitian dollars.

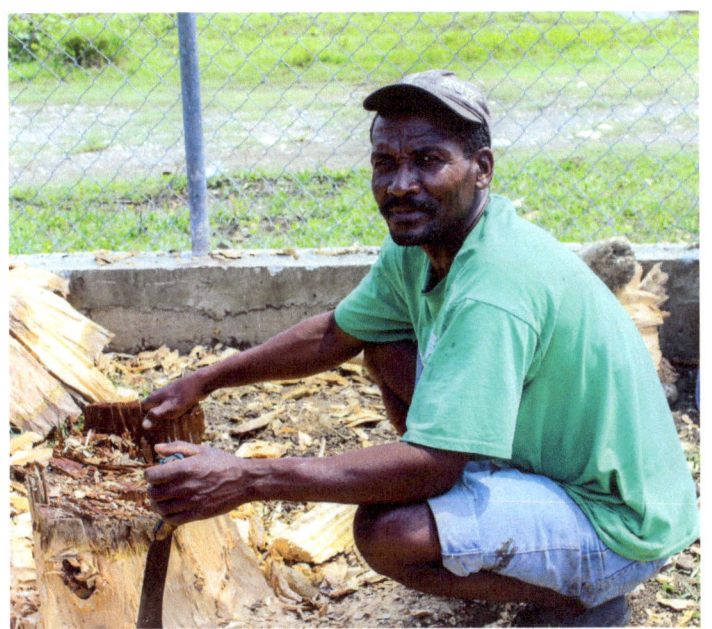

Photo // Jean Marc Fontaine

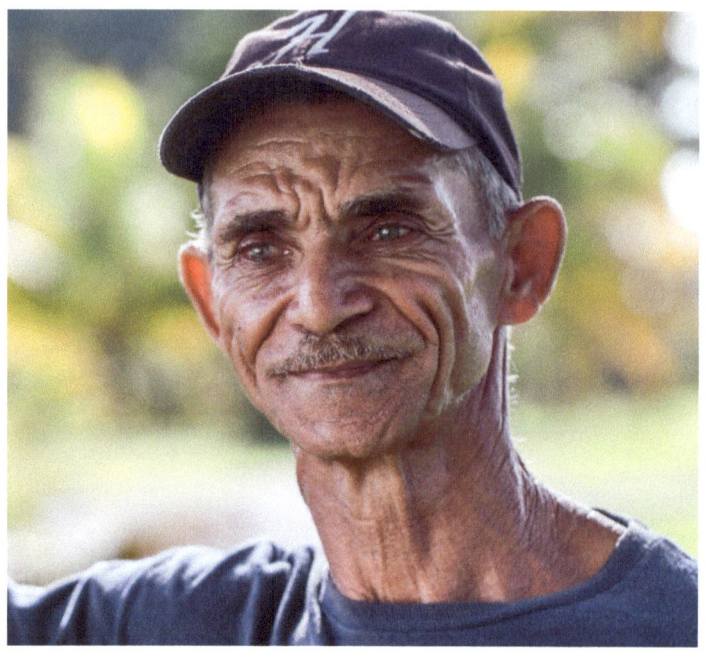

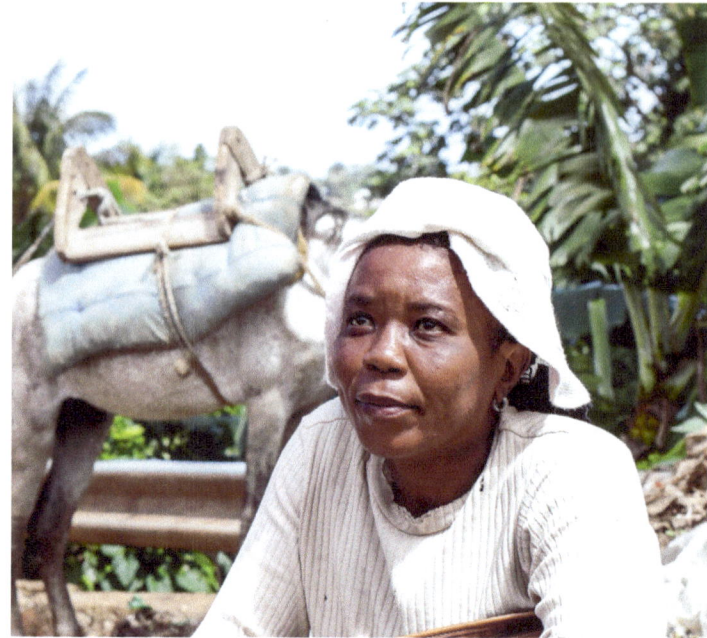

Farmer, Manuel Liriono, 65 years old

Street Vendor, Santhia Filex, 38 years old

I am a farmer. I started working in agriculture because of my father, he was a farmer. I went to an agricultural high school in the Dominican Republic but I moved to Haiti in 1990 and I have been farming here ever since. There is nothing too difficult about farming in Haiti. I also teach agriculture to local Haitians who are interested and want to learn. The problem with farming in Haiti is that some people care about it, but some people do not. On a typical work day I wake up at 6 am, and depending on how much work I have to get done I will finish around 5 or 6 pm.

I have been doing this street vending job since 2012. I used to sell different materials, but now I sell rice and other beauty supplies. I like this job.

I leave my house at 2 o' clock in the morning. I live far away up the mountain and it takes three hours to get to the market from my house. I walk to get there and carry all of my things with the help of my horse. I buy and resell things.

I have two children. One is 8 years old and the other is 6 years old. While I am at work, they are in school. I have a husband and he is a farmer. He farms rice and corn.

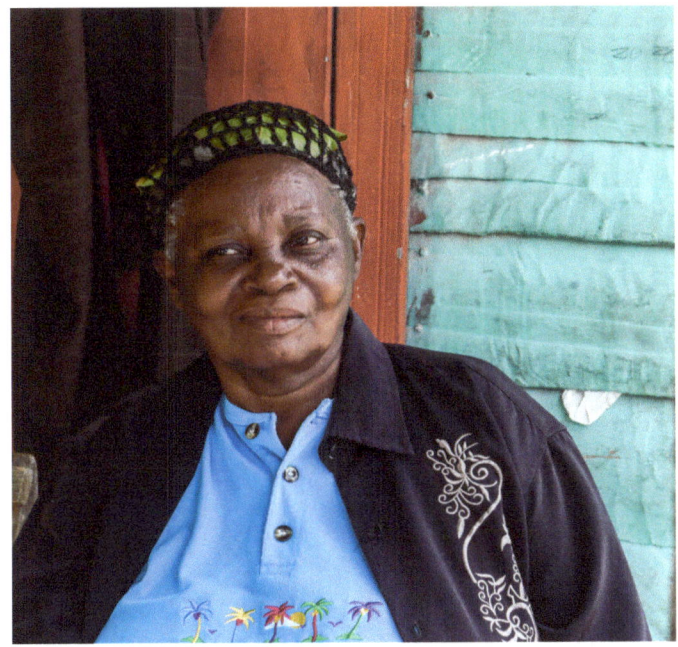

Photo // Shayna Brodsky

Teacher, Micheline Veillard, 61 years old

I teach pre-kindergarten 1 in Haiti, I have 32 children in my classes. I have been teaching for 20 years and I have always taught at New Missions school. I love being a teacher because I can earn money, and I am able to give children education which gives them a brighter future.

I became a teacher with the help of my husband. He was a director at the New Missions school I teach at, so I went to school to learn how to teach and after my schooling was finished I got the teaching job.

The Haitian education system can be discouraging because there are a lot of hard things to deal within the system, but the biggest discouragement is there is no access to the necessary teaching materials. The thing that would make the system better would be having the right type of people filling the teaching and directing positions. They need to be patient people to be teaching children.

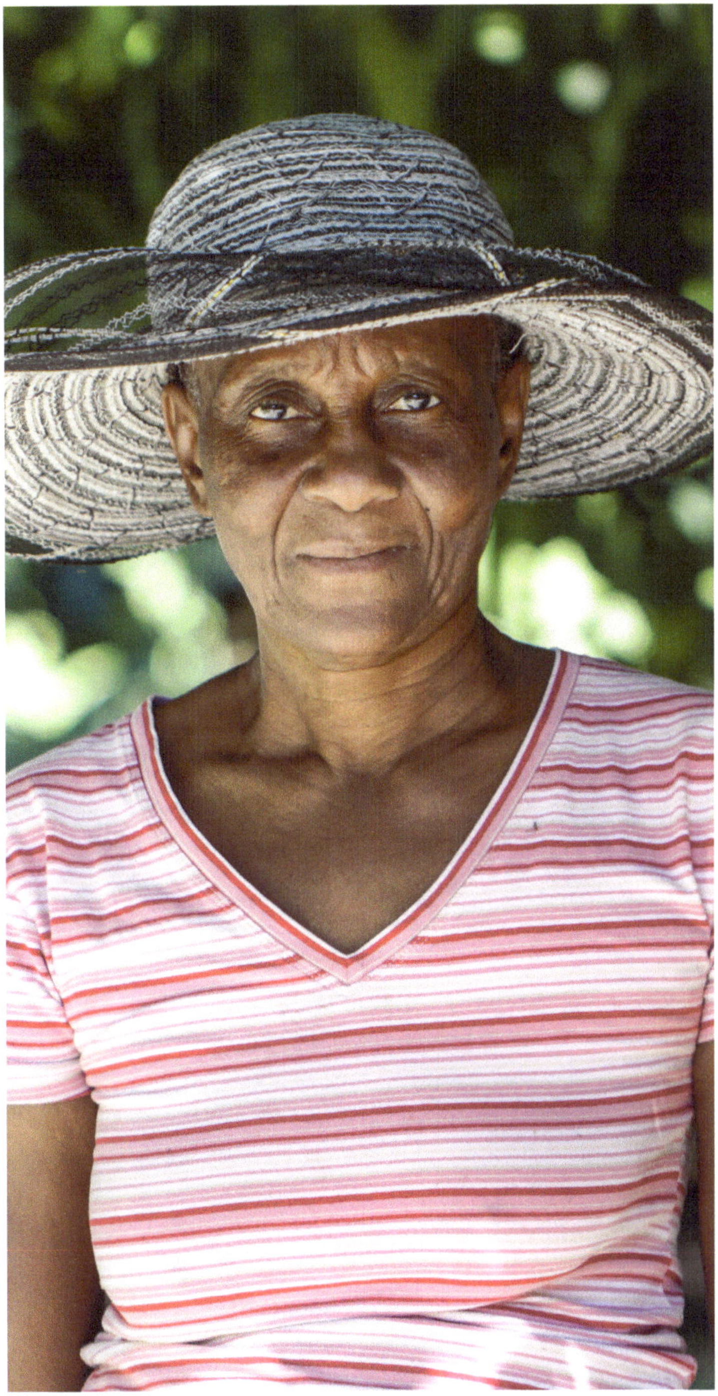

Photo // Shayna Brodsky

Woodworker, Nioben Milus

I started working with wood after I finished high school. I didn't find any other work and my friend showed me woodworking. For a while I worked with my friend and helped him out, one day he saw my intelligence so he allowed me to work at the shop on my own.

Woodworker, John Willce

How I started in [the wood working] business is my father and older brother did this too. I was born in it, I like it, and it pays the bills.

We work at this woodwork shop located on John Brown Avenue, city of Budhan, Haiti. On a normal day there are more than just us two workers here, but since it is Easter Sunday it is just us, and we are finishing up a project.

We both live close to the shop so it takes us about 5 to 6 minutes to get here in the mornings. On an average day we work until we get tired or until the sun goes down. There is no set work schedule, and we do not work for anyone. We are self-employed.

Some people will put in orders if they would like specific items made for them, but if we have the money sometimes we will go buy the supplies and do the work and wait for someone to purchase the item. We earn our money by doing projects. It doesn't matter the amount hours we put into the project for payment. We get paid when the customer picks up the product and hands us the check.

Financially the biggest problem is that we don't have the money or capacity to do the work we would like to do. We love the work but don't have the tools to get it done.

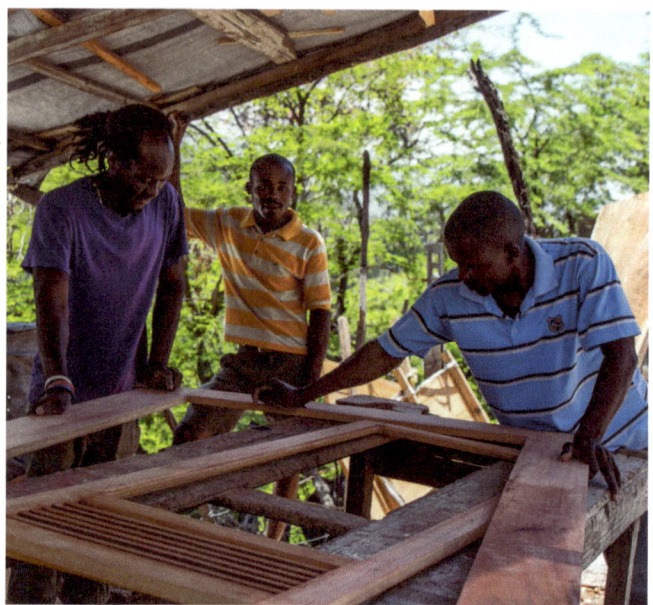

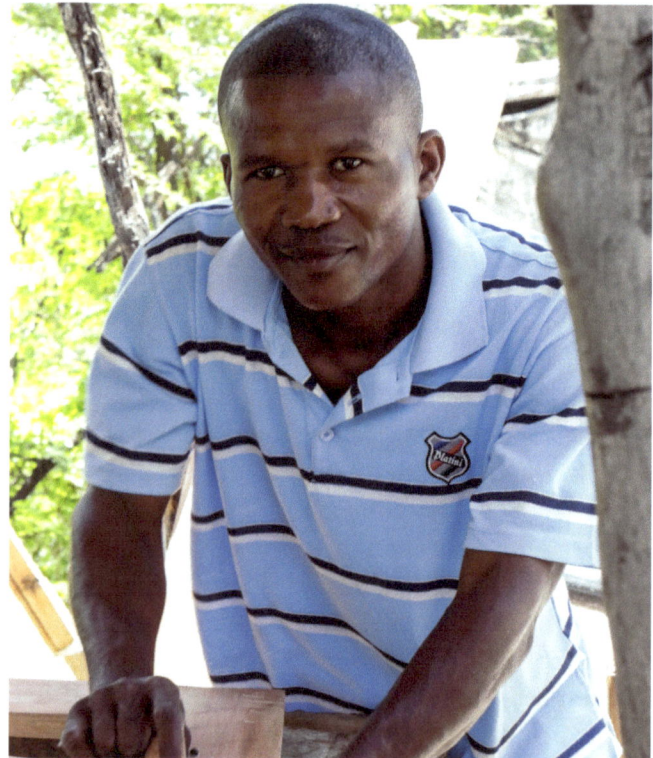

Photo // Jonhathan Burkhardt (top), Shayna Brodsky (bottom)

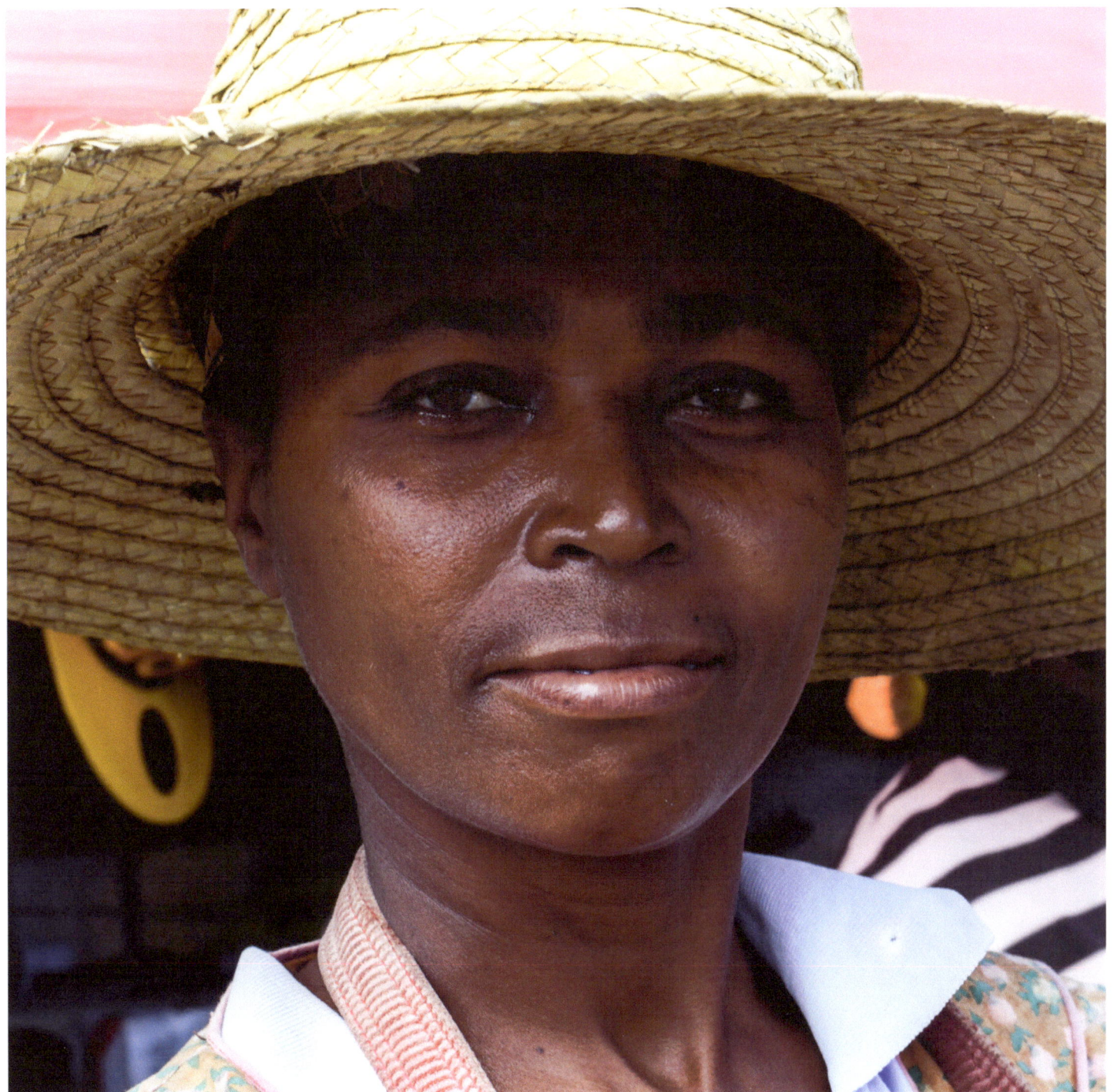

Tiny Hands

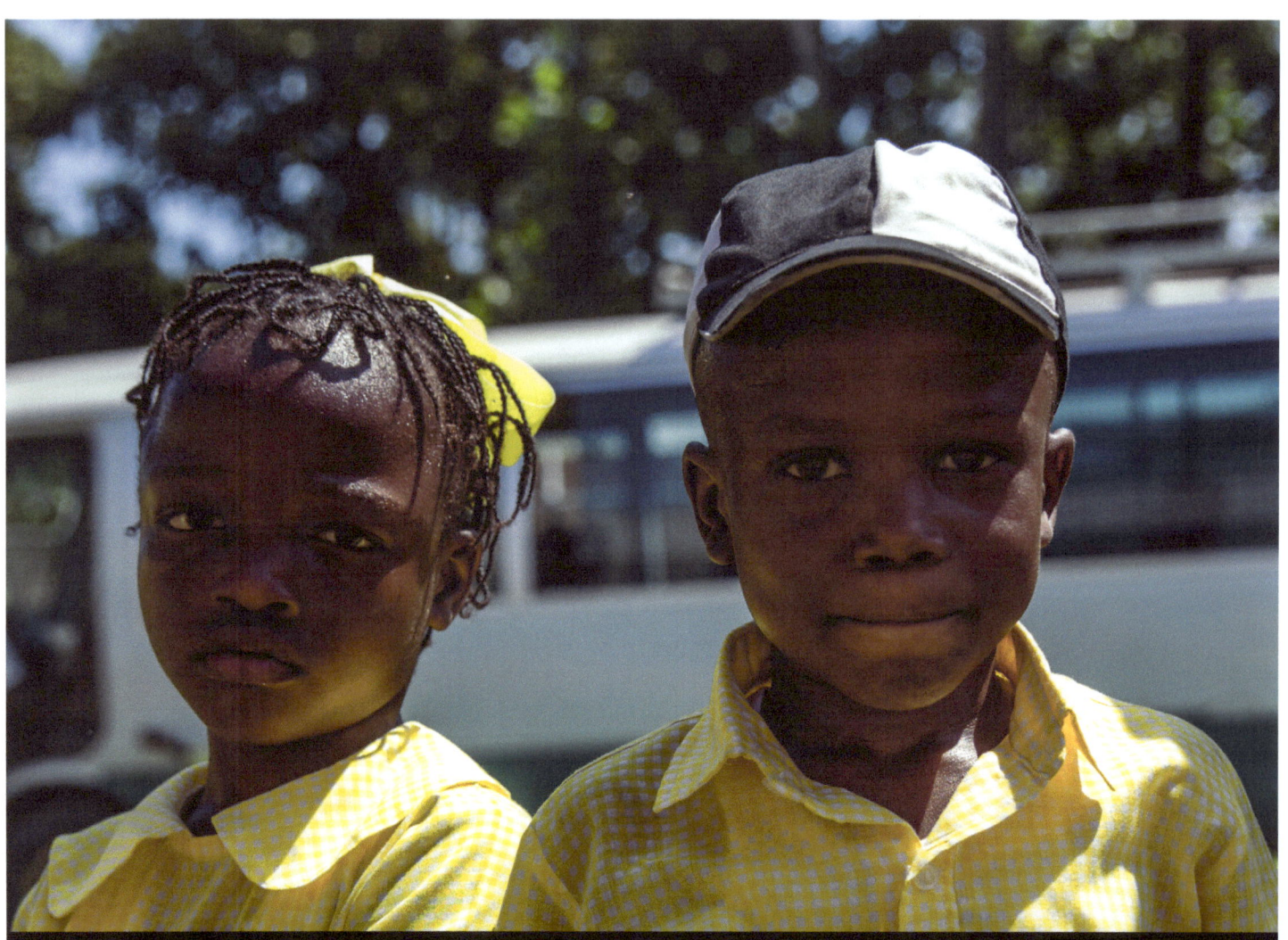

"We really need to put our heads together and do what our motto says [L'Union fait la force]. It's not an easy work doing, but needs a start anyway."

- Larson

Photo // Jonathan Burkhardt

Chapter 8
Education

Haiti has topped a list of the world's worst places to be a school child. A report from the Global Campaign for Education, backed by organizations including Education International, Oxfam, Plan, Save the Children and VSO, warned that poor countries are teetering on the brink of an education crisis with the growth in access to education now stalling.

Nongovernmental organizations, churches, communities, and for-profit operators, with minimal government oversight, privately manage more than 80 percent of primary schools.

If you walk into a Haitian school, you will most likely see rows of hard, wooden benches in front of a dusty old chalkboard. There won't be lots of decorations or colors. The room will most likely be very hot and muggy. The students will be arriving on an empty stomach, some not having eaten for the past couple of days. There will be no electricity, no lighting, no toilets that flush, and a limited amount of textbooks.

Surveys conducted by the UNDP indicate that Haitians who are 25 years and older received on average only 4.9 years of education and only 29 percent attended secondary school. Critical thinking is an important asset to have in nearly any situation in life. As humans, our thinking can tend to be biased, distorted, and uninformed. According to the Foundation of Critical Thinking, "the quality of our life and that of what we produce, make, or build depends precisely on the quality of our thought. Shoddy thinking is costly, both in money and in quality of life. Excellence in thought, however, must be systematically cultivated."

The children here are not encouraged to think for themselves or be creative whatsoever. During class, the teachers call out to the class and students repeat the answers back in unison—a form of learning called recitation.

This is why many of the adults do not think for themselves and become so reliant on handouts. They aren't thinking of ways to recycle or create self-sustainability because starting from a very young age they are never encouraged to think outside of the box. They are trained to be afraid of speaking up. Kids in Haiti are in the third grade and still don't know how to spell their name. They are often beaten in the classroom, as many teachers in this culture passionately believe in physical punishment. This form of education is raising adults that don't take initiative. It creates a group of people that believe they cannot do things on their own and believe that the *blanc* is the solution. Children need to be able to express their ideas. They need to be encouraged to try new forms of thinking. That is why doing things such as art projects and thinking games are very beneficial.

"I like reading the material by myself better. American schools actually use the objects and show us the objects that we are learning about. Big schools in Haiti don't have

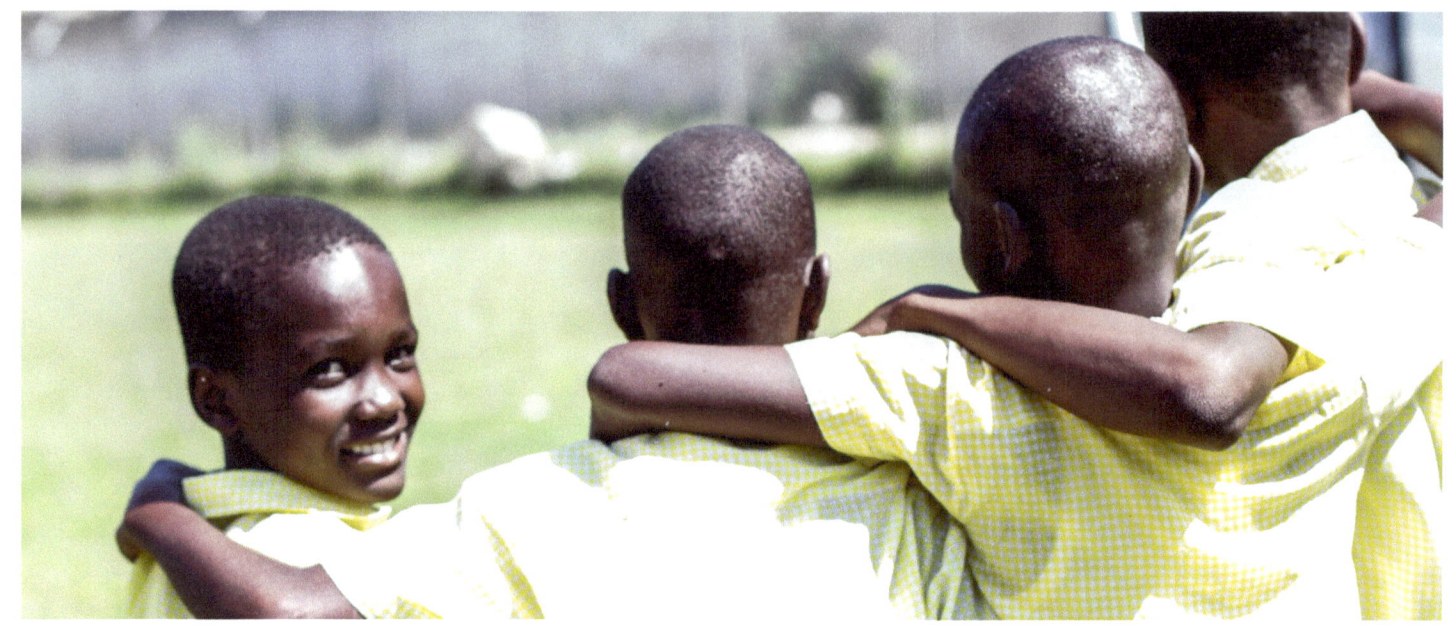

those materials," said Larsen, an 11th grade student at the New College Concordia.

What is really beneficial is when international teachers partner with Haitian teachers to empower each other and share knowledge. Often when short-term missions teams come, it is purely so that they can gain an enriching experience and feel good about themselves. They usually like to see a tangible change that they made such as a building they built. Sharing knowledge will last for eternity.

According to Steve Hersey, director of Quisqueya, an international, American run school in Haiti, in Haitian-run schools, students are not used to being asked their opinions. Their opinions typically aren't valued.

"Students who transfer into our school are a little mystified by the fact that we would ask them what they think about a piece of art, literature, or music," he said. However, they tend to be good at memory.

"We celebrate diversity and alternate solutions. We want students to contribute more to their own learning instead of being just given a list of facts to memorize," said Hersey.

Many Haitian students, even the fairly well educated ones, don't read books- only excerpts and articles. Even college graduates don't have access to books like we do. Even the really good Haitian schools don't value creativity as much.

"For me being a student in Haiti is not easy," said Juloveney Etienne, a 21-year-old Haitian student at the Port-au-Prince University in Haiti. "It would be better if we could have more materials and have more practice to see things in reality. It would be a better education than that of memorization."

Haiti's rote memorization system came from the French. "You'll often hear kids chanting facts in classes," said Hersey. It's very difficult to analyze when you are used to always just needing to know the facts. "The amount that can be memorized is amazing," said Hersey. "It's impressive. They can memorize pages, but asking them what it means gets you into trouble."

Also, in Haiti, your look is very important. When entering most school buildings, everyone is always looking his or her very best. Clean and polished shoes, crisp suits, perfect dresses. If a little girl doesn't have bows in her hair perfectly, she may even be sent home.

Education in Haiti is a way to get out of poverty or to advance in society and get a better job. Lots of families make huge sacrifices to send one of their children to school, much less all of them. However this is where the problem comes in. Because of how much they value education, there are a lot of schools that operate as "businesses that prey on poor people," as Hersey called it. They accept money, raise funds, and often do not deliver. This approach to education does not increase the child's chances, but the parents don't know that. They are desperate and their kids can get into these types of schools more easily. There are many schools that are operating purely as profit operations, without the oversight of a board.

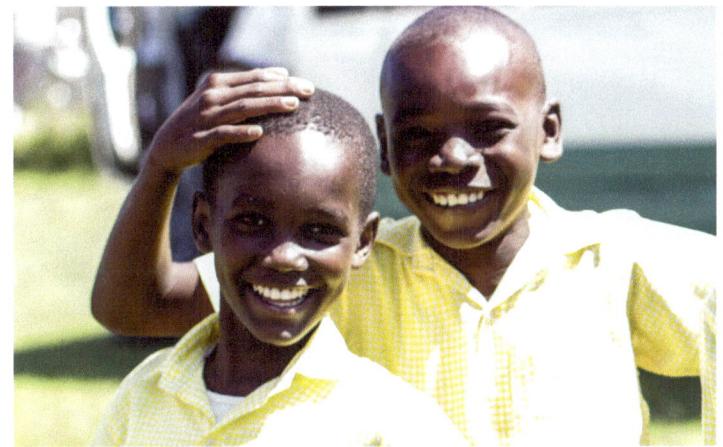

There is a very strict national curriculum that Haitian schools follow and very regimented national exams that all students must pass in order to advance to the next grade level. Schools start on a certain date and will get closed down if they don't follow that. At most schools, students must pay a large percentage of family income in order to go there. On top of this entrance fee, there are other added on charges for uniforms, school books, and more.

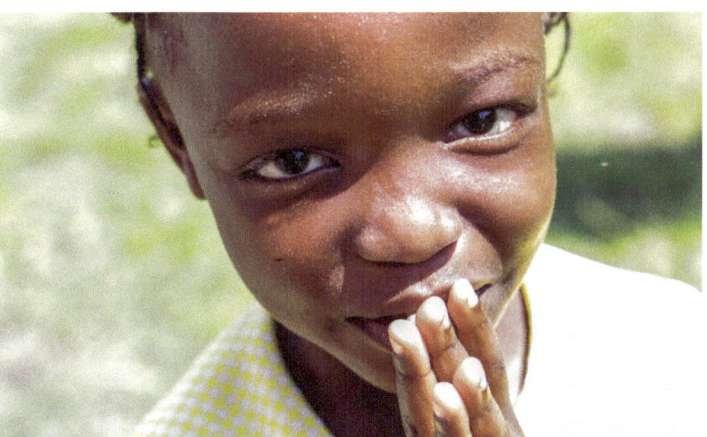

One of the biggest controversies within the education system in Haiti is whether the schools are being taught in the French language or not. Traditional schools in Haiti are typically taught in French. French tends to be seen as a higher language in Haiti. However, there is a growing

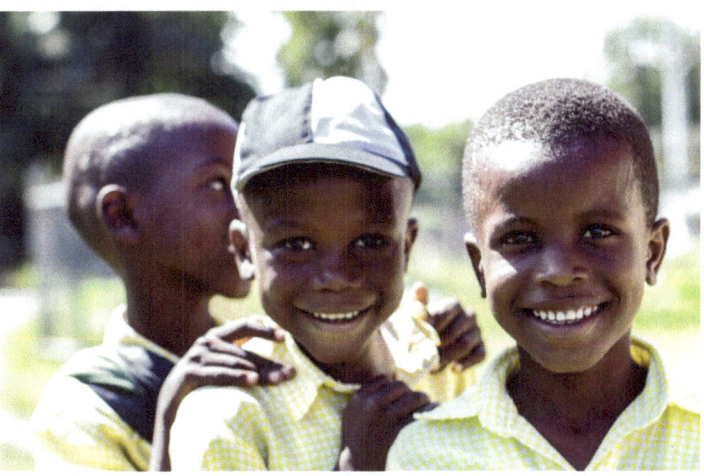

Photos // Shayna Broadsky

movement to start off teaching in creole and transition into French later. French is a second language to a majority of the population in Haiti. That's typical in Haiti- to start speaking a little bit of French to establish one's status and show that one is educated, and then slip into the language of the heart. Having the education in French is holding people back and excluding them from the system. Only very recently have schools started teaching in Creole. French is seen as a means of advancement. Some people are very against the teaching in Creole. It's one of the social issues. Some kids in upper class are punished for speaking Creole. "That's a language for the maid," some will say. Some kids end up going to school anyway, and then not understanding much. The French being used in the classrooms sometimes may not even be that good. However, Creole is just as advanced as French. One can discuss business, physics, philosophy, anything any level in Creole. It is a fully developed and beautiful language, Hersey said.

What the education system in Haiti really needs is more materials in Creole. And the students need to begin learning at a young age in Creole because it is the heart language of Haiti. According to an article by Hurisa Guvercin a mother language has a very powerful impact in the formation of the individual because the child is getting familiar with the sounds of that language in the womb before even being born. Guvercin says that a child's psychological and personality development will depend upon what has been conveyed through the mother tongue.

With that being said, they need to veer away from the rote memorization. They don't need to leave it entirely, because there are some aspects of teaching in French that are good. However, they do need more divergent thinking.

Because there is a huge lack in access to ongoing teacher training, there is a tendency for teachers to become complacent in Haiti. Or, some teachers simply don't have much training to begin with at all.

"With the average Haitian school, you have well meaning good people doing the best they can," said Hersey, "but their education level might just be notch above the students."

Something that makes life at school easier are the things that most Americans take for granted, such as drinking water, toilets that flush, computers or even electricity. In the majority of Haitian schools, these commodities can be difficult to find.

"We need more materials to teach the kids better," said 31 year old female teacher Vilarson Gilberte who teaches Pre Kindergarten 2 and has been a teacher for 11 years at the New Missions Elementary School in Leogane, Haiti.

Another huge issue is the empowerment of women in the schools. According to an article by Helena Cicmil, thousands of the country's women and girls continue to be threatened daily by gender-based violence. After the earthquake, many women were forced into tent cities where they were subject to sexual violence. In the majority of Haitian households, women are in charge of all of the chores, cooking and childcare. With the exception of well educated parts of Haiti, the culture is for the most part patriarchal. So many Haitians have a sense of entitlement that is seen in the way that female teachers are treated.

In conclusion, the education in Haiti is so crucial because if the children are raised correctly in the classroom, they can grow to be a people with hope. They can be prepared to face all of the challenges awaiting their country. Haiti needs citizens that have ideas to improve the community and living conditions and are actively carrying out those ideas. Creativity in the classroom will lead to initiative outside of it.

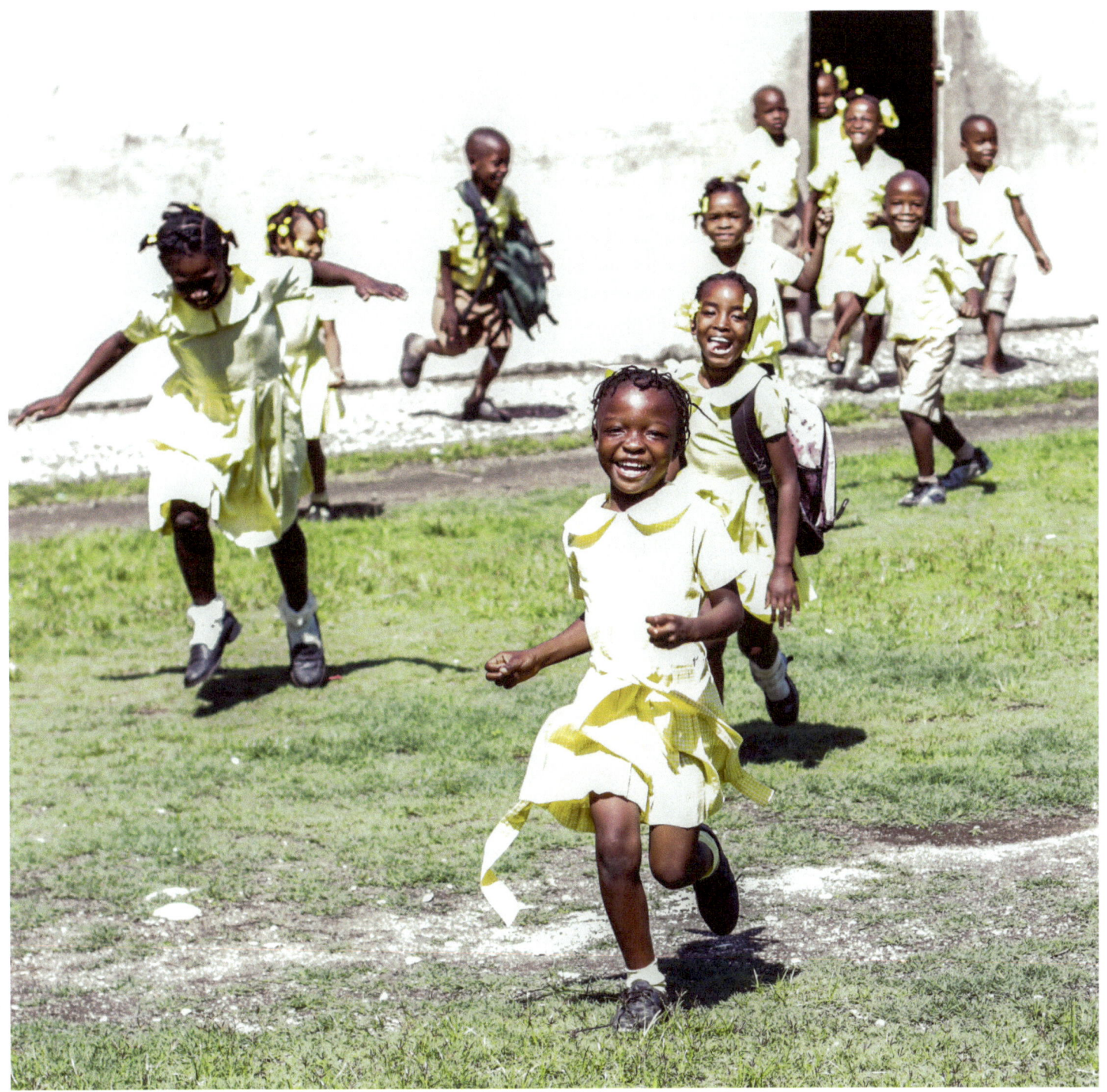

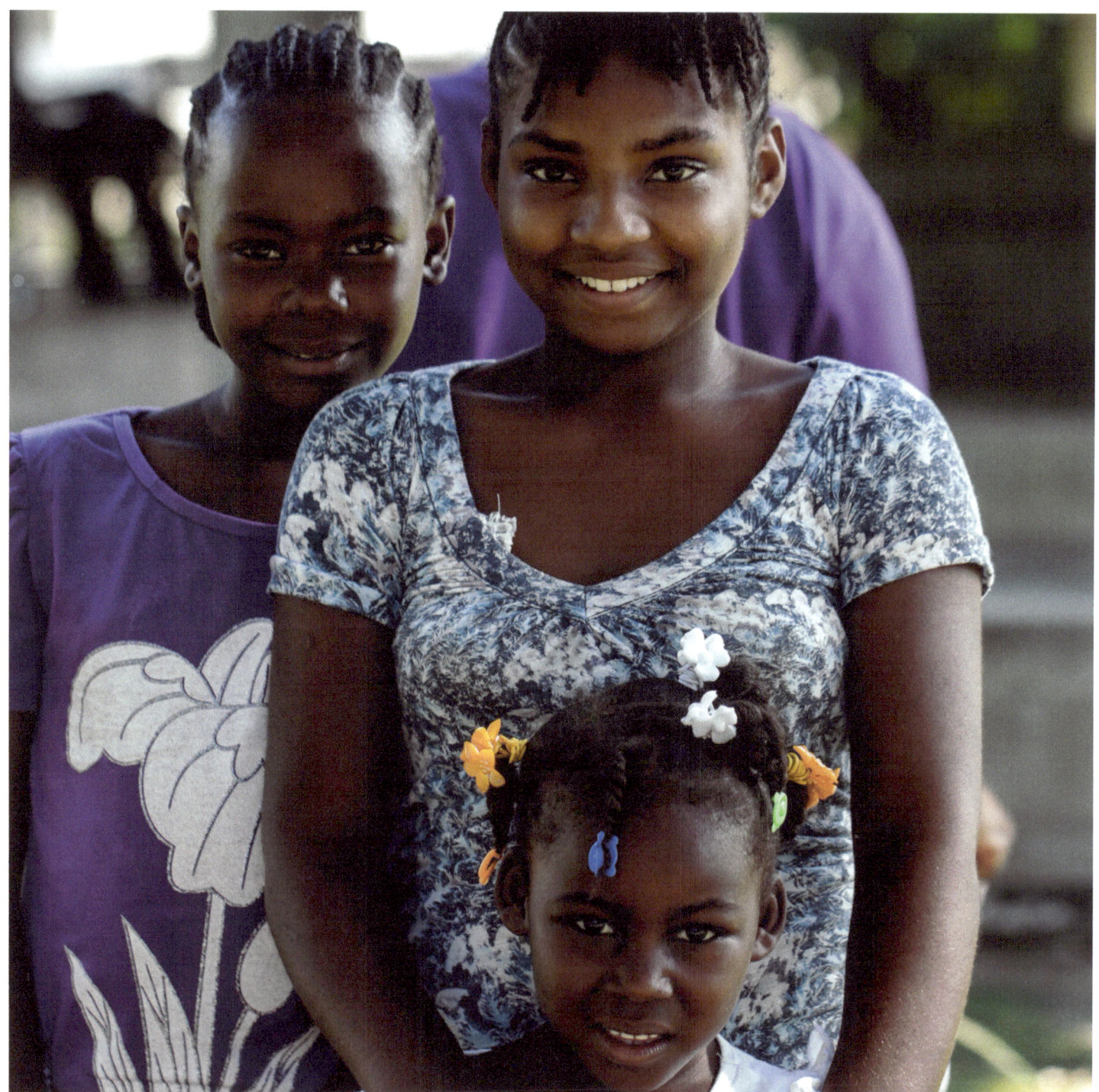

Chapter 9
Family and Orphanages

Broken down

It was extremely hot that summer day in Port-au-Prince. As we were walking around the ruins of the once iconic cathedral, two older Haitian women came up to our mission team, each of them holding brand new babies in their arms. They were talking to us in almost rude sounding tones, and I could not help but notice how they were holding the babies. They held them so carelessly, it looked as if they were going to slide through their loose grips at any moment. The women followed our team around the crumbled cathedral the entire time we were there, and kept repeating their gruff creole phrases to us. As we were getting into our van to leave the women's gruff tones started to sound more desperate. When we started driving down the earthquake broken road leading away from the cathedral, our team leader told us that the women were begging us to take their babies from them. They wanted to just give their children to people they did not even know.

The reason these two women were trying to hand the babies to our missions team is very simple; they wanted these children to have a good life. They wanted to give them opportunities that would not come to them begging outside of the crumbled cathedral. In Haiti there is this misconception that anyone who has white skin is rich so one could guess that these women were not trying to give their babies away because they did not care about them; one could actually argue the opposite.

Family Life

Social class remains a huge determinant of what family looks like in Haiti. Some aspects remain the same—average family size is 4.2, the men are the breadwinners and the women typically tend to the children and work in the household. Divisions in styles of family life begins with class divisions. Upper class families own their own homes and live similarly to American families in regards to having sustainable provisions. Middle and lower class families tend to have multi-generational homes, with much of the extended family living together under one roof. While it seems logical that mothers would have time to care for their children, the responsibility often falls on the older children in the family.

Another main aspect of Haitian family structure is marriage. The most common form of marriage among poorer Haitians is known as *plasaj*, a kind of common-law marriage. Similar to a polygamist marriage, men begin several families with

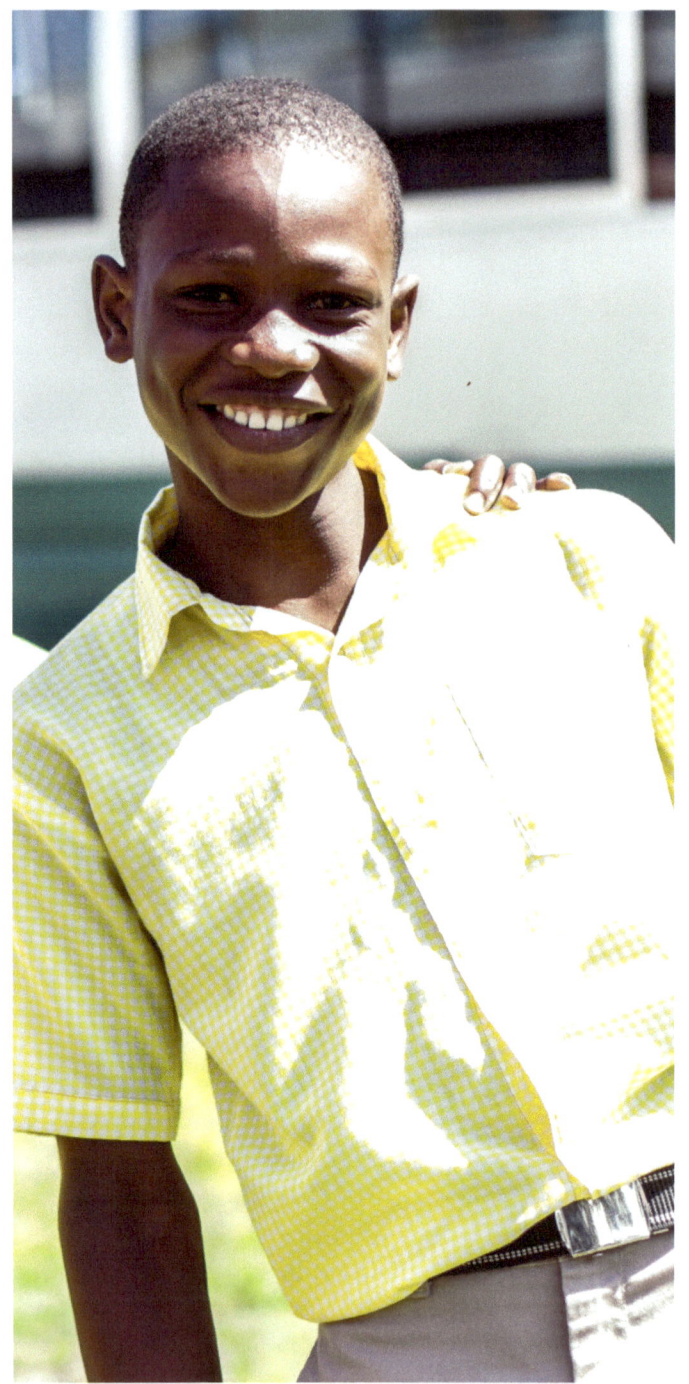

Photo // Shayna Broadsky

different women. This is considered normal in the Haitian lower class families, but still has not been lawfully accepted. Due to the popularity of *plasaj,* many mothers are left alone to support the family as well as care for the children.

According to an article published by ReligionandPolitics.org there are hundreds of orphanages stretched out across all of Haiti. A common misconception about these orphanages is that they are filled with children who are truly orphans, but that is not the case. Most orphanages in Haiti are filled with children who have one or more living parents. The question of why might come up. There are two major reasons that play into why this would happen. The first is it is common in a Haitian family structure to have very large families, having 5 to 7 children would be a typical family size. Also, it is very common for women to have children with more than one man, and for her to be left caring for the children on her own. Also within Haitian culture, women do not have the same job opportunities that men do, so finding a way to provide for 5 to 7 children becomes very difficult for her. This leads into the second reason, that being that the living family members cannot provide for the child. So rather than leaving them on the streets, they give them up to the orphanages.

The Alexander children currently live in Riverside, California, having been adopted by Kermit and Tami Alexander five years ago—right after the earthquake. Their story, in the next chapter, fits right into the orphan misconception. Five of the six children in their Haitian family were living in orphanages but were not truly orphans. At the time they were adopted, both of their biological parents were still living. The Haitian children spent most of their lives in different orphanages around Haiti; however, there were times when they lived with their mother at home. Here are their stories.

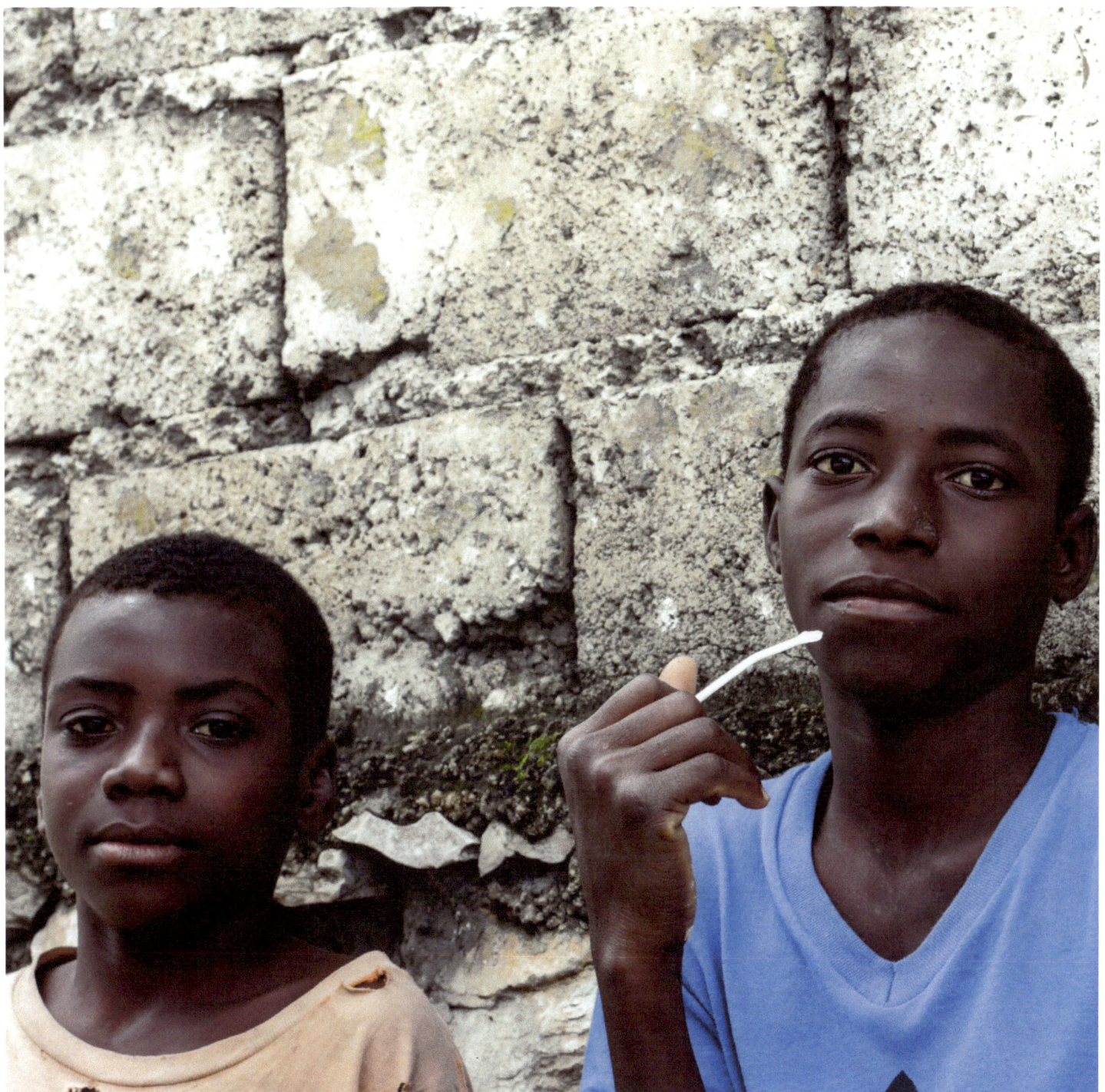

Photo // Shayna Broadsky

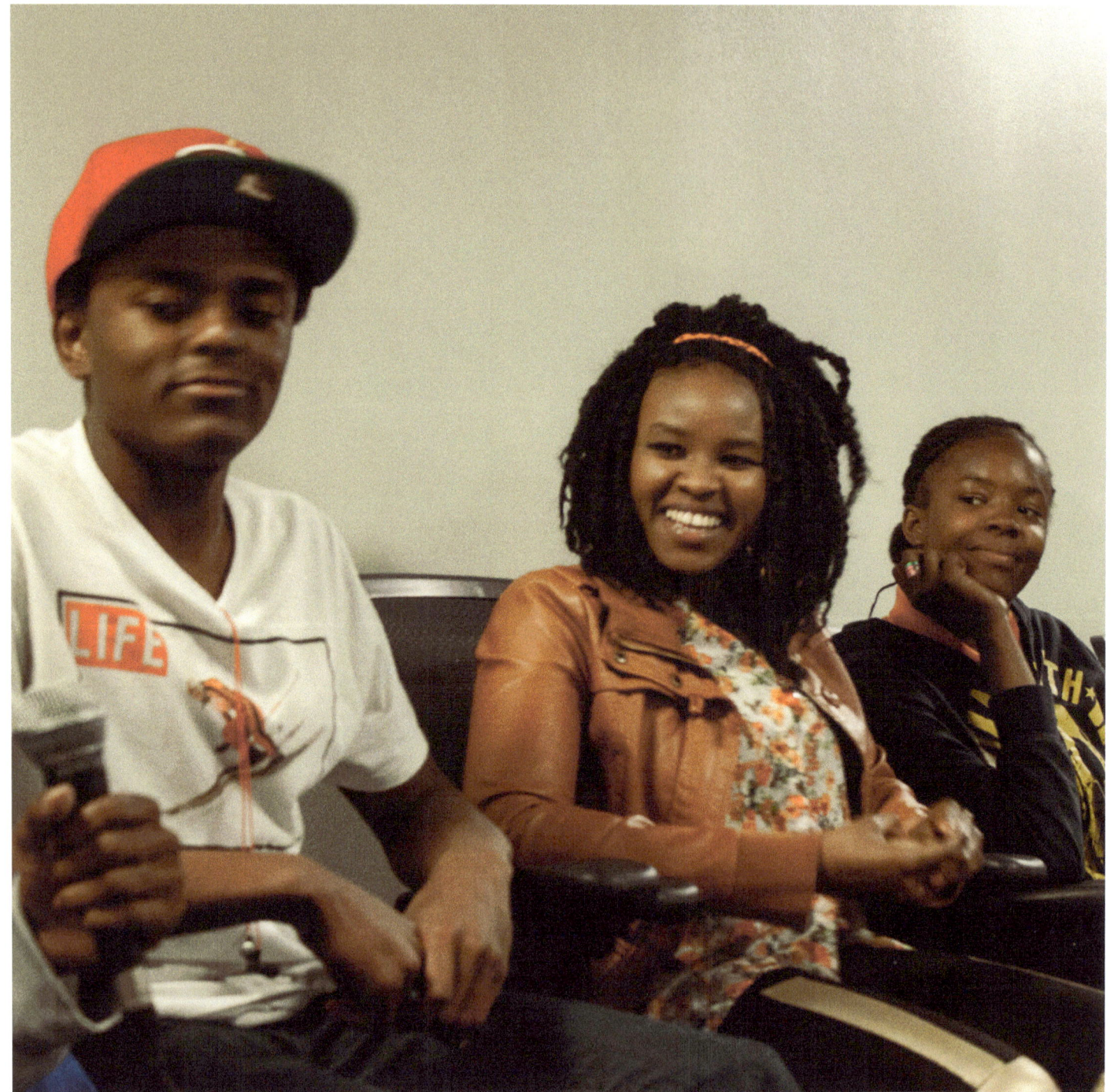

Photo // Morgan McKay

Chapter 10
The Alexanders

Manouchecka, 21 years old

My relationship with my sister, it wasn't really a good relationship with her because I never really lived with her. Most of my time was at orphanages. When I moved out from the house I was young so I did not really have a great relationship with her. Even now we talk, it's like, is it just like my siblings here or no? I never really had a great relationship with her. With my mother it's almost the same too. When I used to live with her, she was always the way that your mom raises you, but she was always sick so it's not that I always sit with her and have a great conversation with her so it's been different. I don't know if I should call it a great relationship.

Both orphanages that I spent my time in, my role was to braid kids' hair. I always enjoyed doing that so it was a way for me to feel happy whenever I do that. The first orphanage I was at, I used to clean the church and mop it. I [would also] wash my siblings' clothes and do everyone else's hair, like the little kids. Sometimes I would also help cook.

We all knew that we couldn't just wake up and sit there. Basically, I would say yes, I had a role, but I actually chose to do what I did, so it was not like I had force to do it. I guess there were other choices that I could pick from I would say. You needed to do something, it's not like you can just sit and not do anything.

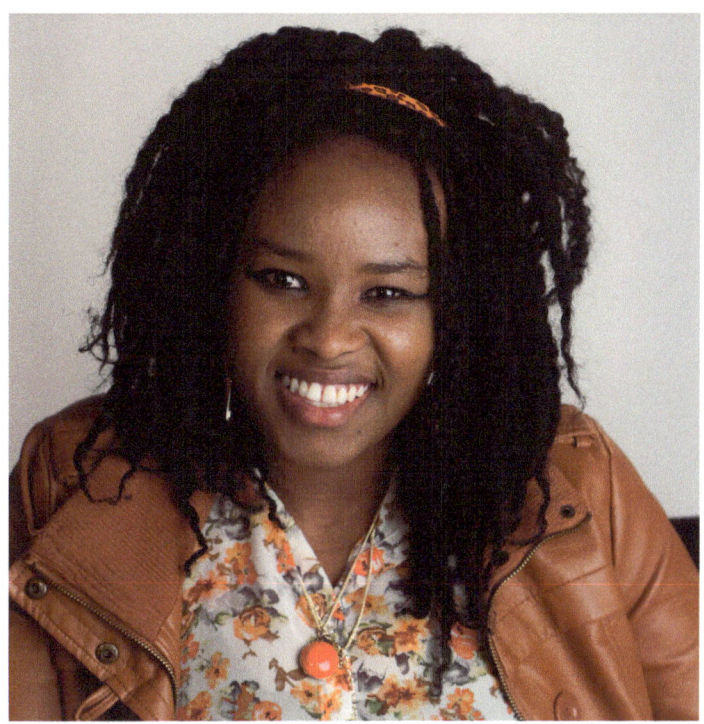

Photo // Aaron Fooks

-63-

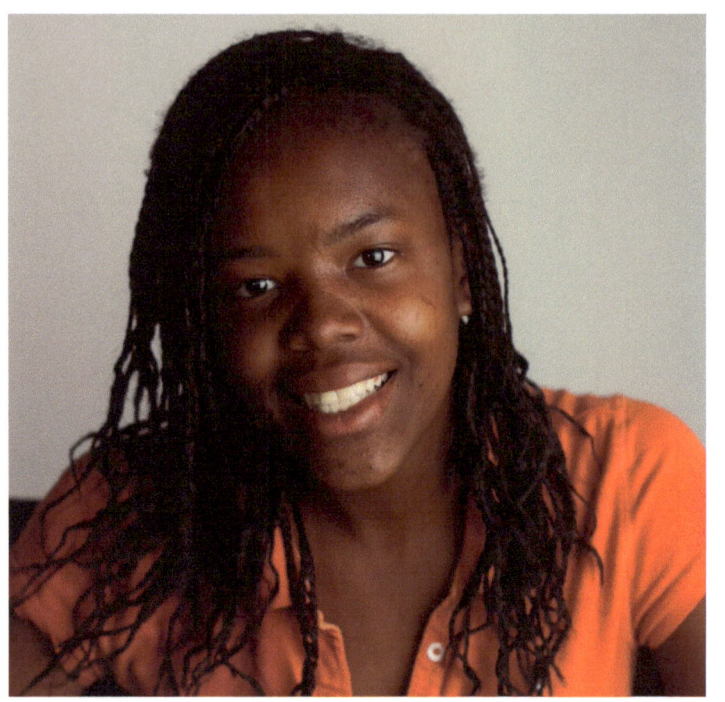

Semfia, 14 years old

I didn't really have a role, but I was more of a helper. I helped kids, played with them, little kids. I always enjoyed playing with the little kids at the orphanage. That's basically what I did.

[The room] was kind of in the middle of small and big. They had seven bunk beds and seven people, seven girls. The room was green. There were windows and curtains.

My favorite memory of Haiti is climbing the mango trees and getting mangoes for my friends because that is my favorite fruit. I could eat mangoes forever. I also liked playing dolls with my friends at that time. Sometimes some of them would make their own clothes for the dolls. I like making doll clothes too. Now that I came here, I don't know how to make them anymore.

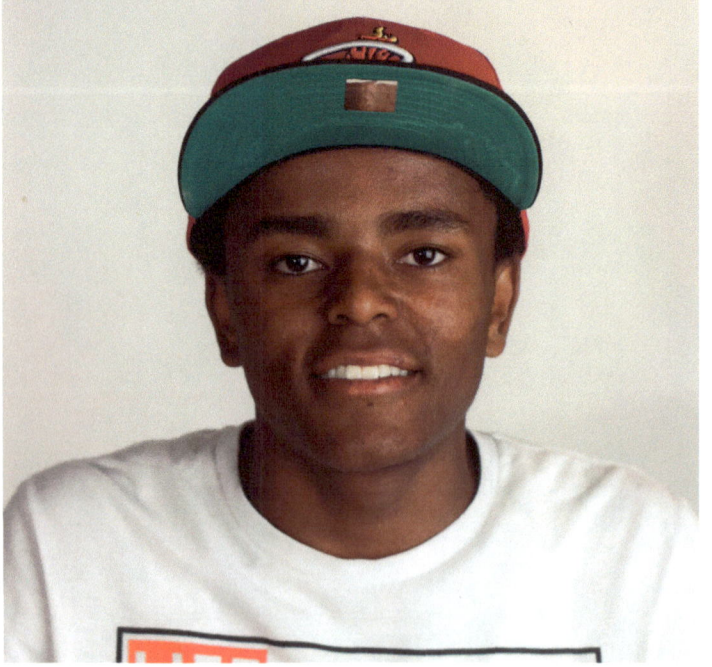

Clifton, 17 years old

Mission of Hope was the orphanage I was in. It was great, just playing with kids. They had messages throughout our lives that they taught us—to be a good man and a man of God. We had three things we could do—play basketball, ride bikes and hang out with friends and play soccer. They had an education that was so great. They teach you a lot of stuff, how to be important and how to move on in life and be whatever you want to be. It was a good experience having missionaries over all the time and them helping us be successful.

There were a lot of people in the orphanage that really influenced me. I would say Rachel and Brad were the most important people. Everytime they would come when you were feeling bad and try and make you feel good, try to impress you and whatever they could do, they would pick you

Photos // Aaron Fooks

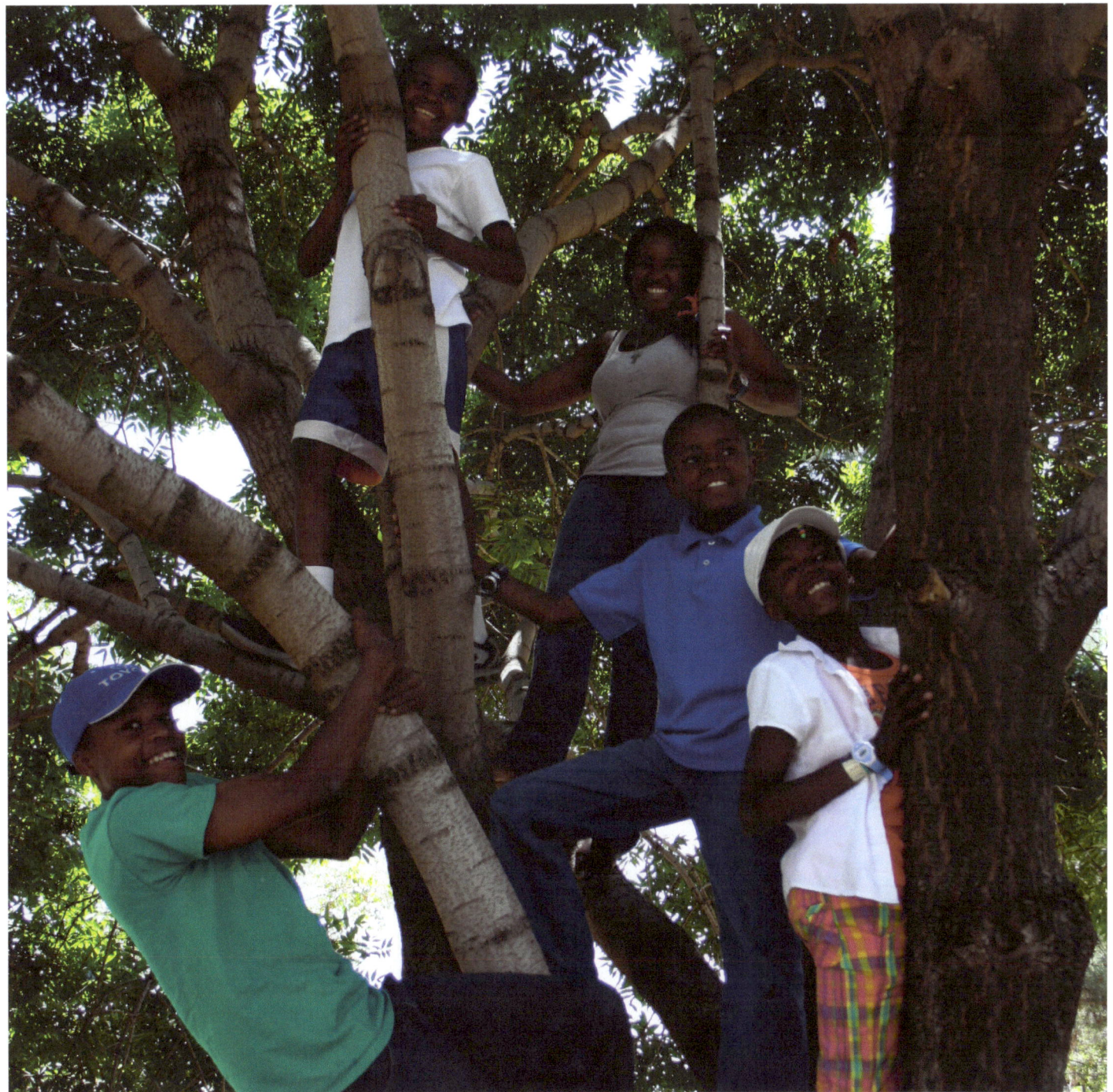

Photo // Tamra Alexander

up in whatever you were struggling at. Also Tony, who was one of the kids in the orphanage. He was one of the young adults in there. He would know what we were going through because he had been through it already. As a young man, he would make us feel proud, feel good about ourselves for being in the orphanage.

Because we had so many kids, our responsibilities were to clean our room, clean our bed. We had seven people in each room. They had one room clean up the kitchen, one room clean up the yard. As we went on, we signed up to do specific things. I would be cleaning the dishes and someone else would clean up the tables. The first responsibility was to wake up, go to school and clean up your room. At night we would do the chores.

We went to school 365 days a year. We did have summer, but it was the same as going through school because we were doing the same things, memorizing the Bible, playing soccer or basketball, its pretty much free time in school but we weren't doing homework.

I would say [my favorite activity] was playing on the team of soccer or basketball. Back then, we would be competitive just playing, even in something that doesn't count.

The thing I miss most is hanging out with my friends. They were down to earth and would just play with you. Here [in America], it's like, 'whatever'. In Haiti, you would ask somebody and they would be like, 'yeah, I'm down' whenever, no matter what time it is. They just wanna play with you. It's not like, you go to the park and nobody's in the park. In Haiti, you go to the park and they will accept you and you will just play with them.

I was a troublemaker. I think my best story was at my second orphanage, Mission of Hope. I remember a time when we had finished dinner and we didn't have enough, we were still hungry. There was a storage room where there was powdered milk. There was a group of guys that were hungry, and we all went in there. The door was locked, and from our room to the storage room there was the wall that separated [the two rooms]. We climbed up on the bed, to the top of it, then went over it. They threw me over it because I was the smallest. I got the box and threw it back to them. Then I heard a voice, and I thought I knew nobody was in there, but then the supervisor was in there. I was like, oh gosh! She was like, "what are you doin'?" I said, "the ball went over there, I was just trying to get it." "What's the box you just threw over to the other room?" "Oh, yeah I threw the box over there." She went to the other room and found the other five guys over there. She got us down from there and got us outside with the box. She said, "see what those guys just did?", she was talking to the whole orphanage, "see what those guys were doing when you were out there playing?" I felt ashamed. She got us out in front of all the kids and she had all five of us stand in a line ready to get whooped. One of the kids, the oldest one so nobody could have called him out, said, "oh, I was just walking in the room and saw these guys and I didn't have anything to do with it, I was just looking at them." Nobody could have called him out so he left us in the struggle. Nobody said anything about it, so he was out and we had four other people who had to stay and get a beating.

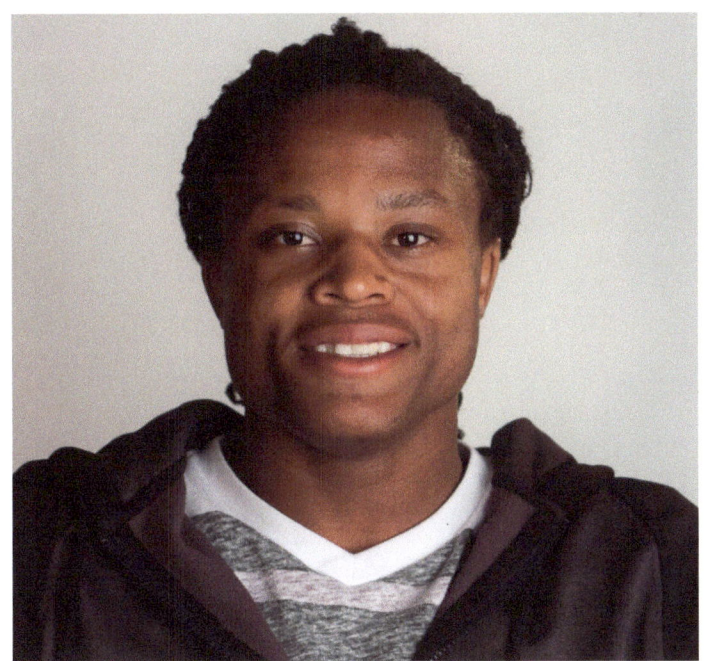
Photo // Aaron Fooks

Jameson, 19 years old

My dad was a farmer so growing up I looked up to him and how he grew his own food. When my mom was sick and she couldn't take care of us and they put us in the orphanage, from there I brought the skill that I saw my dad had with me. When I was in the orphanage I started planting and making my own little garden. It transitioned into a bigger role in my life, where I could focus on doing my garden without getting in trouble, just relaxing my mind by doing the gardening work. I got very good at it. In Haiti we have more freedom to do a garden. We can sit and look at them, and when they are finally starting to grow, that's the exciting part. Compared to here(California), where you have to go to school or go on vacation, sometimes we have to let another person water it for us, but if we don't have that person, we come back and it is almost dead.

I didn't really spend that much time with my dad. I knew who he was because most of my life I was growing up in the orphanage and he would come visit us and bring food for us but honestly I didn't have that great of a relationship with him. I knew who he was but I didn't really have that father and son connection.

I was super young and his garden was behind the house, so I could see what he was doing. I would look at what he was doing and capture it, and I wanted to be that when I was older. My dad and mom actually lived with us for a while. It was in Port au Prince where we were all in the same household.

I was a small kid [when I was in the orphanage]. The most I got out of the orphanage was to be patient and somebody will always take care of you as long as you do what you're supposed to. I was a little troublemaker, but it happens when you live with a big group of guys and you have limited space. It gave me the opportunity to look at it as a long-term process and just know that one day I will eventually get out of it and try to make something out of nothing. That was the orphanage for me, just part of a long journey, that's how I view it.

In Haiti, when we were in the orphanage, we had mango trees everywhere. We couldn't go out, they locked the gate. So I went in the back yard and climbed over the gate to get mangoes from the mango tree and tried to get back, but I put my head over and they caught me. I had to drop the mango like they told me, and I got a spank.

Future of Haiti

Srafina Melo

Medle Doniste

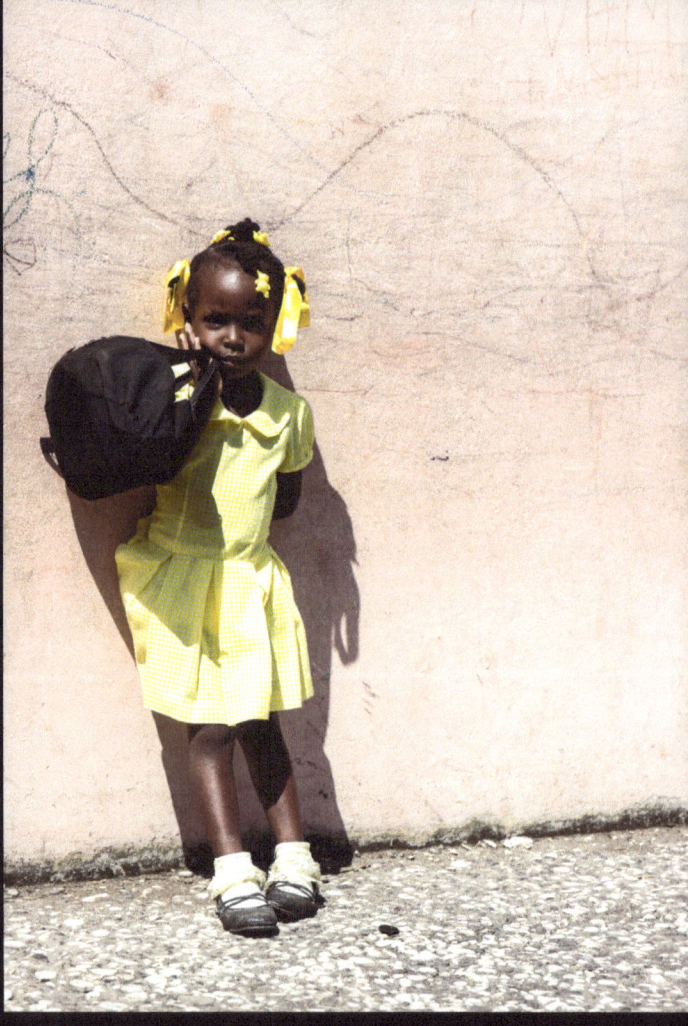

Photo // Johnathan Burkhardt

Photo // Shayna Brodsky

Little Sratina has dreams of becoming a business woman when she grows up.

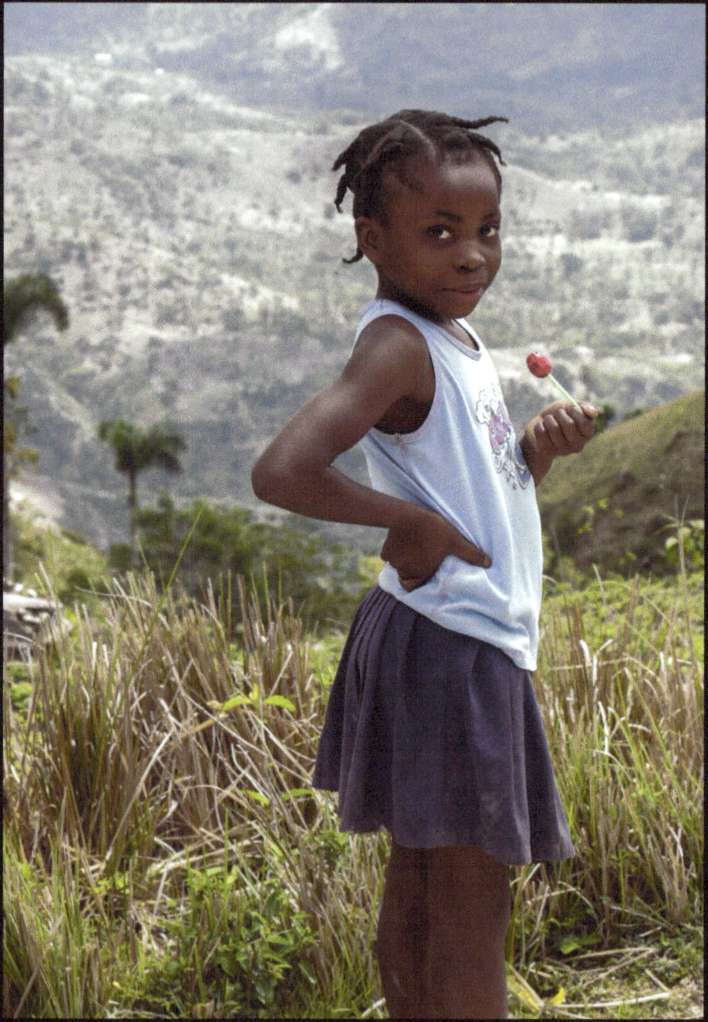

Six-year-old Medle loves learning at school and wants to be a business woman when she gets older.

Christel Walter

Jeffery Gioto

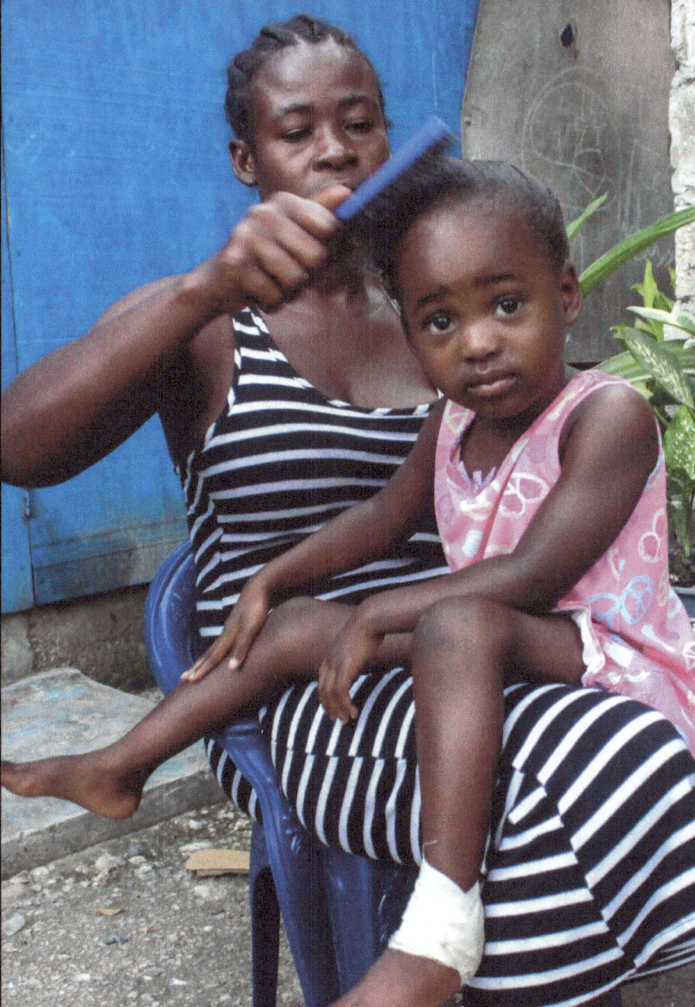

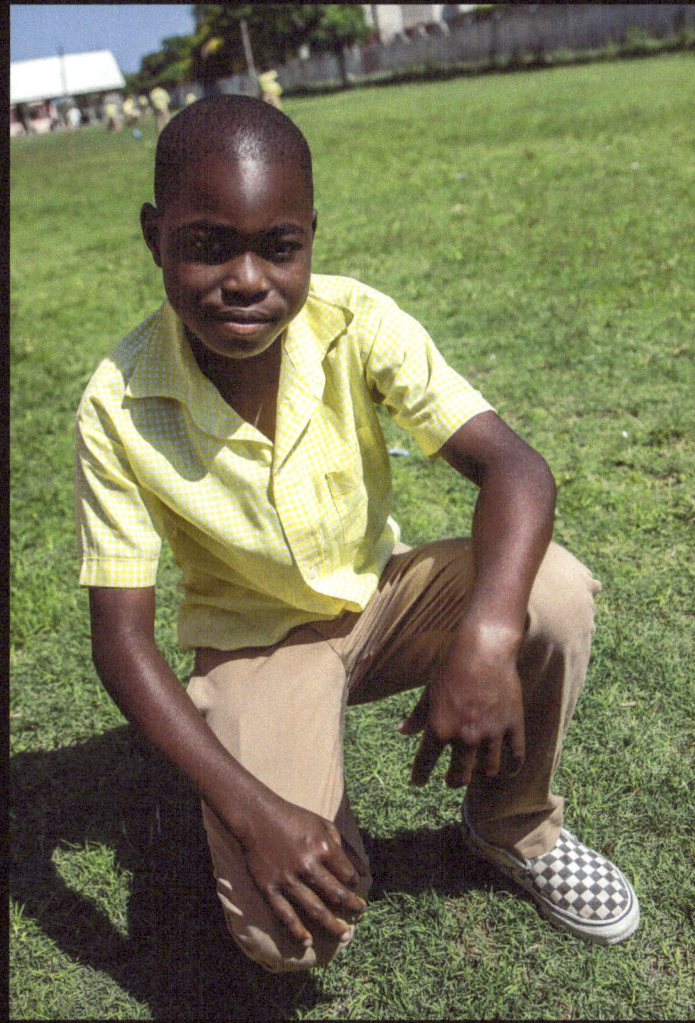

Six-year-old Christol loves school.

Six-year-old Jeffery likes school and wants to study math when he grows up.

Wilkensly Deisir

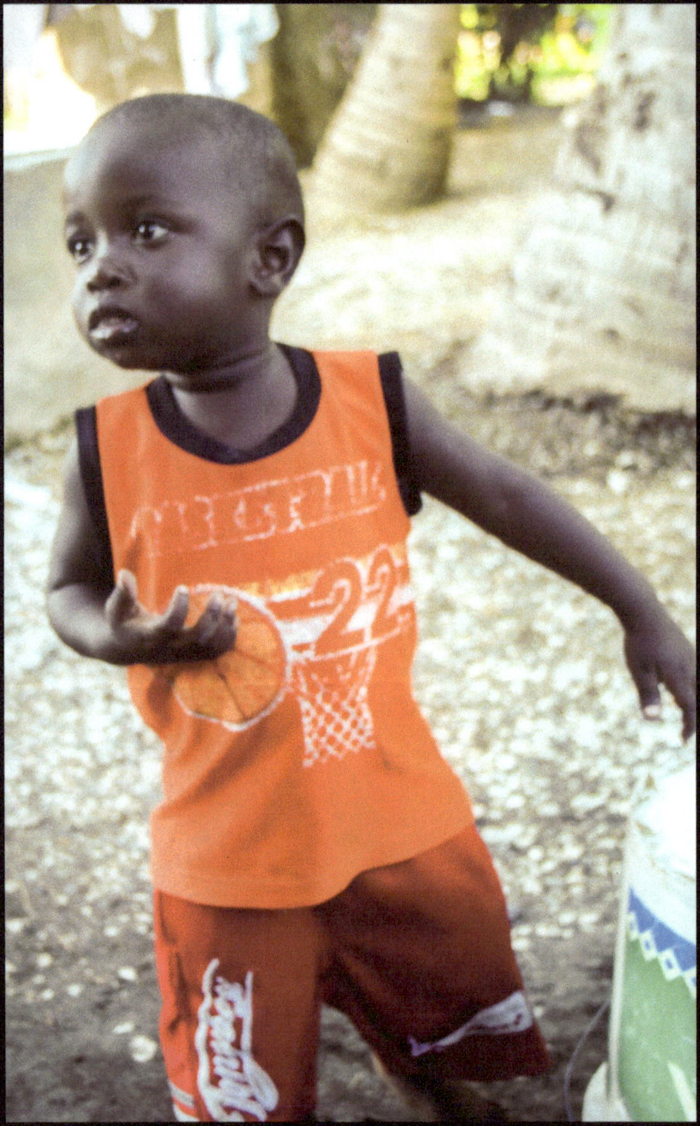

Photo // Delopherne Fabrice

Three-year-old Wilkensly is just starting school and loves to learn.

Maneyssa Edourd

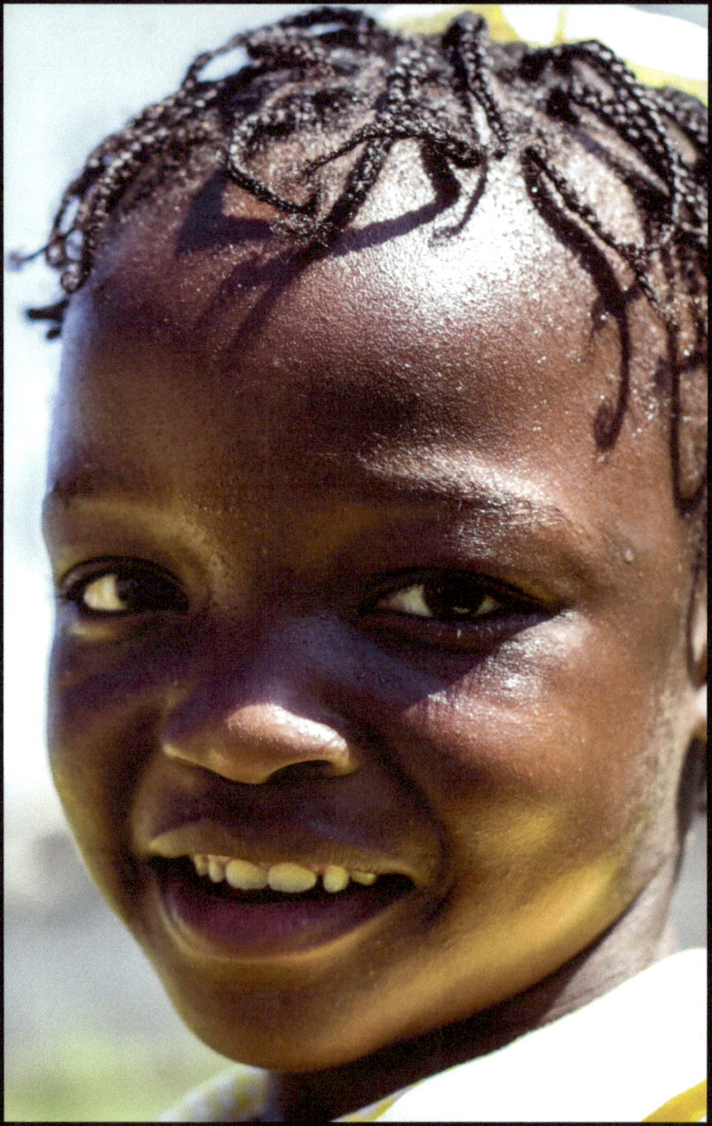

Photo // Shayna Brodsky

Six-year-old Maneyssa likes school and wants to study math.

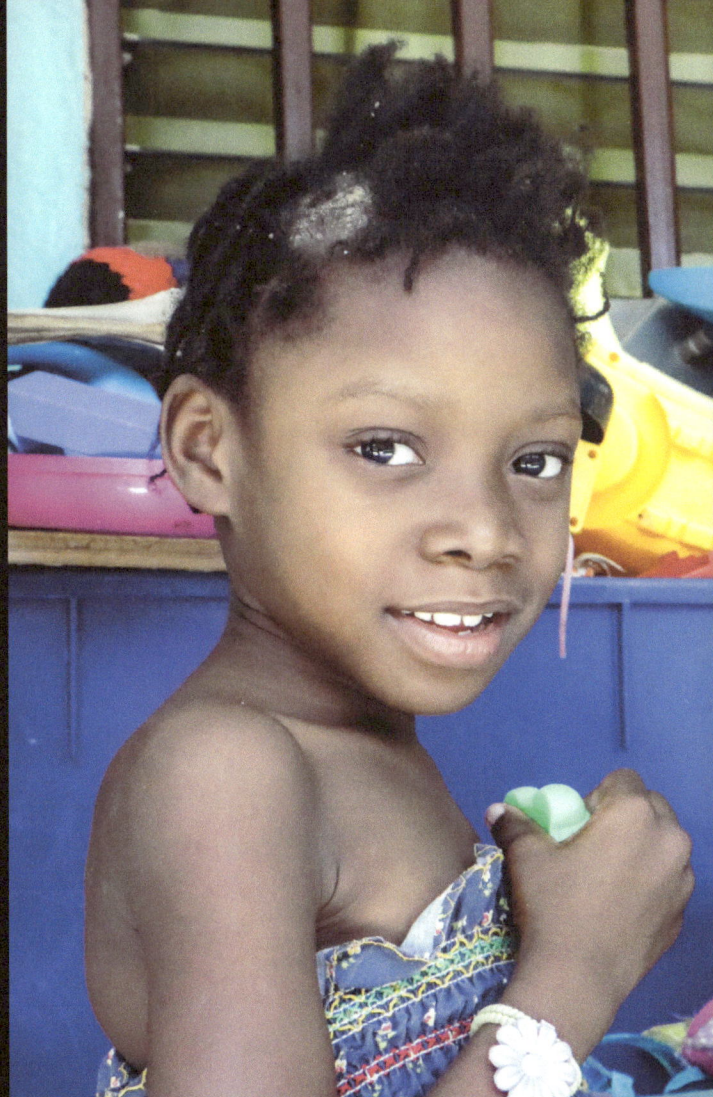

Photo // Shayna Brodsky

Frendli wants to be a nurse when she grows up and do surgeries to help people.

Contributors

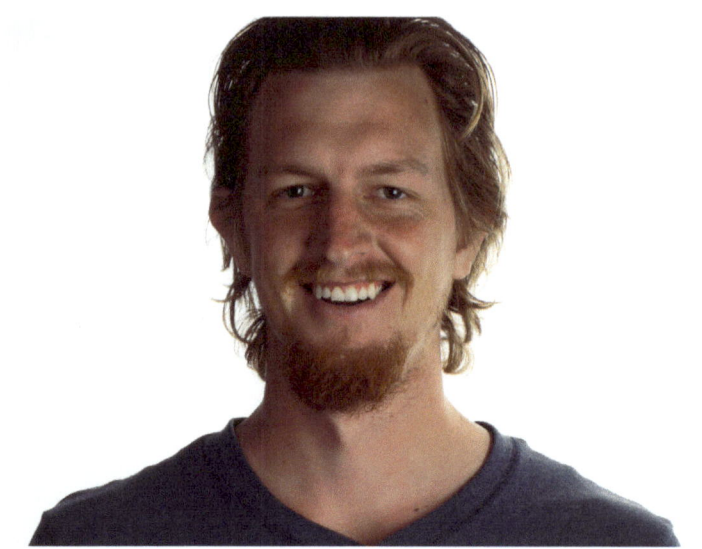

Johnathan Burkhardt
Senior Editor

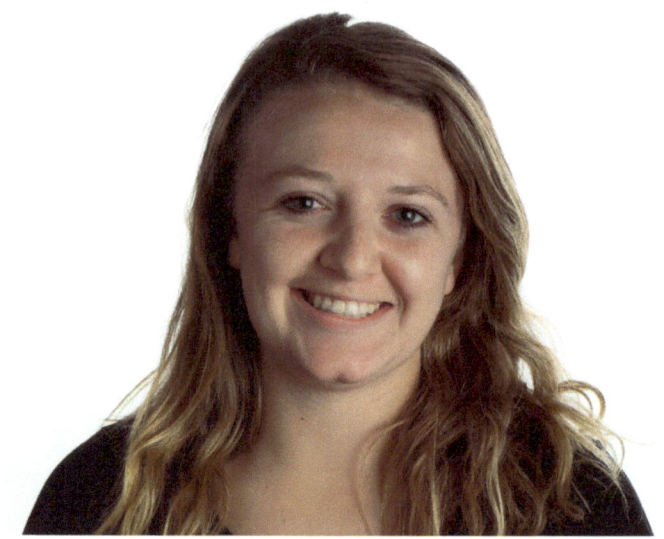

Ashleigh Fox
Visual Editor

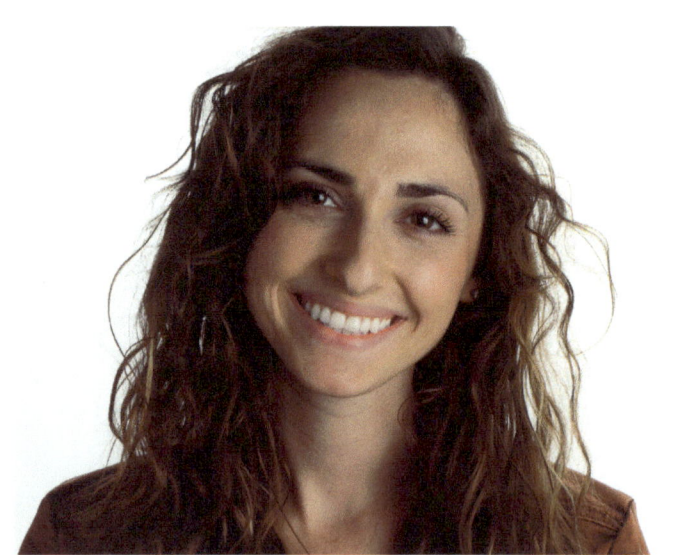

Shayna Brodsky
Writer & Photographer

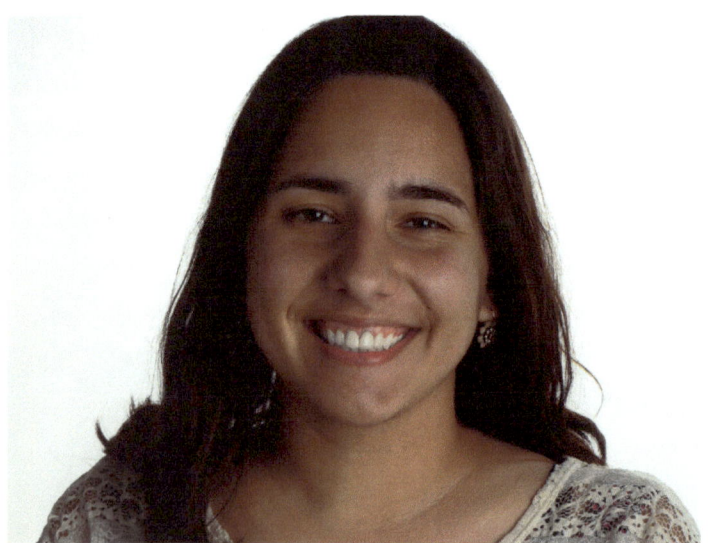

Nicole Foy
Writer

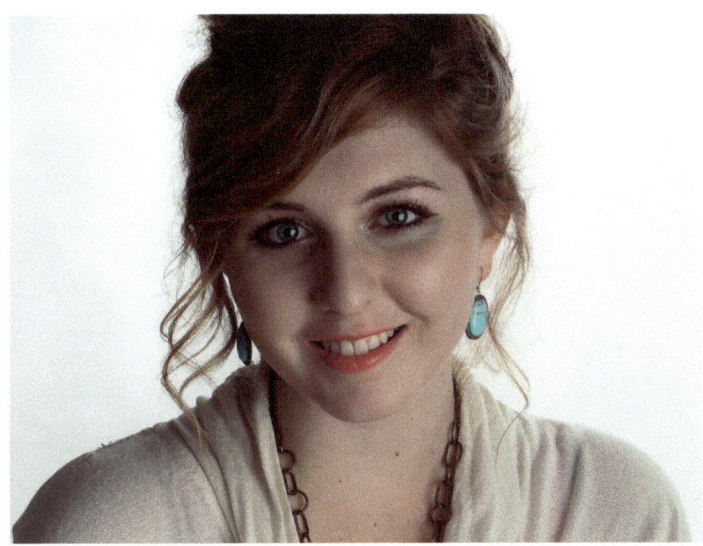

Rachel Allan
Story Editor

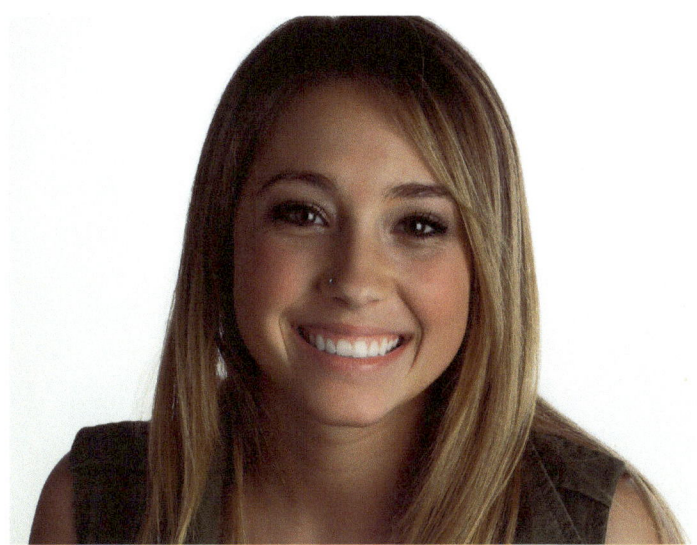

Chelsea Wiersma
Writer & Photographer

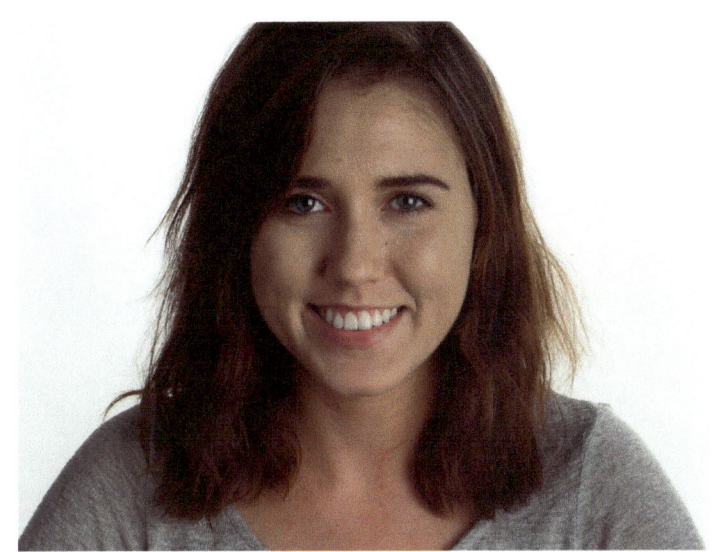

Torie Hamilton
Writer

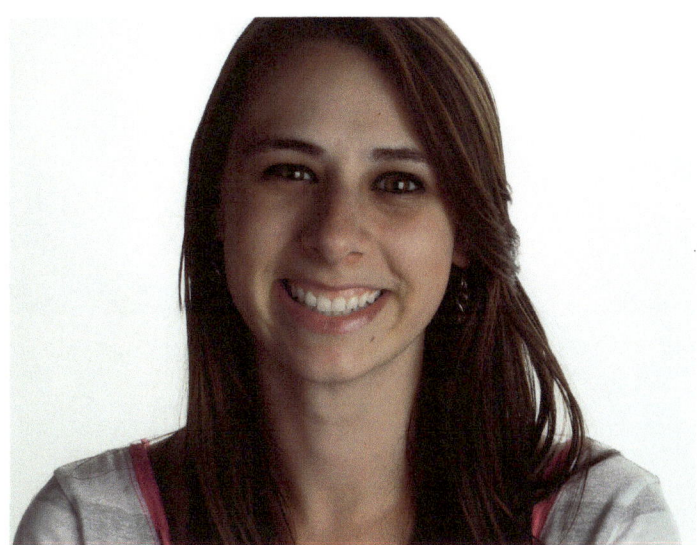

Nicole Mojarro
Media

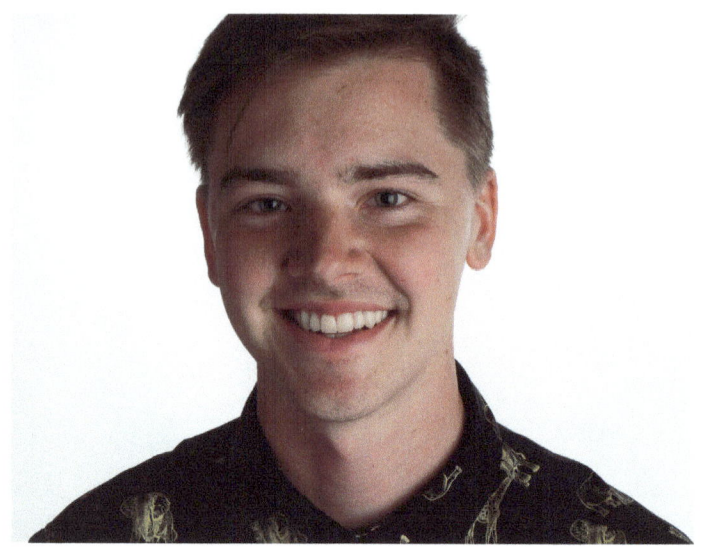

Aaron Fooks
Photo Editor & Designer

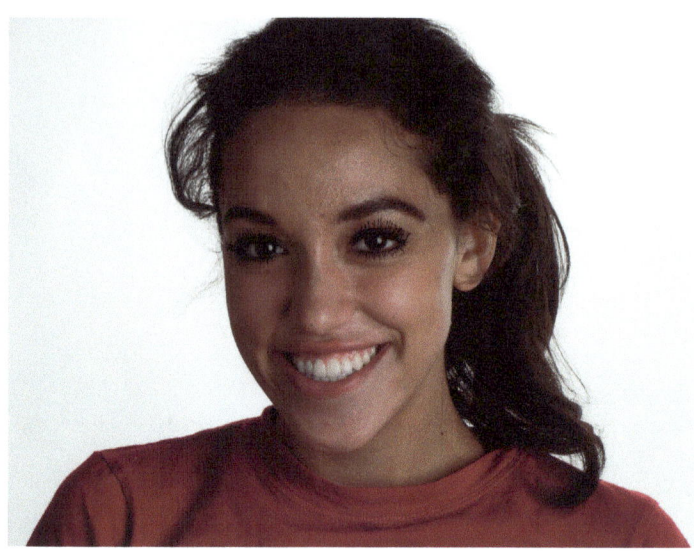

Morgan McKay
Media

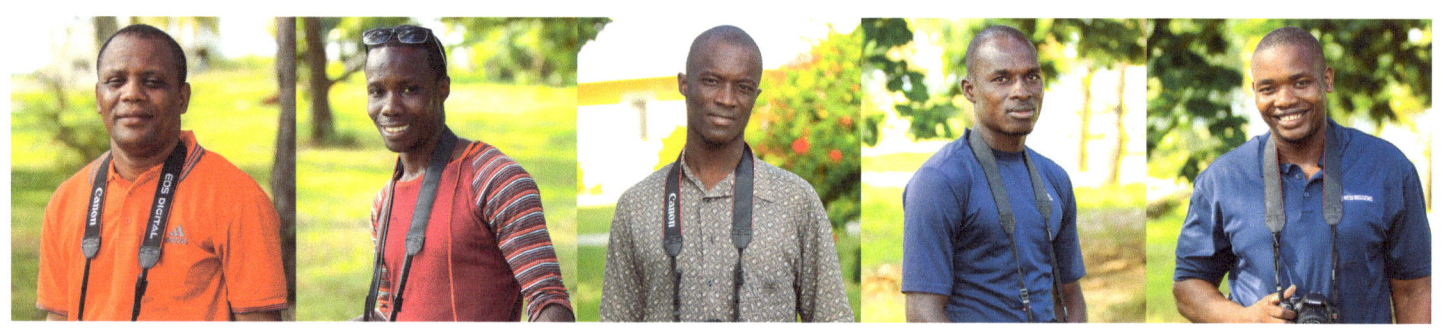

Harold Rene
School L'acule

Widnel Cerisier
School Santo

Hoselio Jean Jacques
School Darbonne

Delopherne Fabrice
School Calouitor

Jean Marc Fontaine

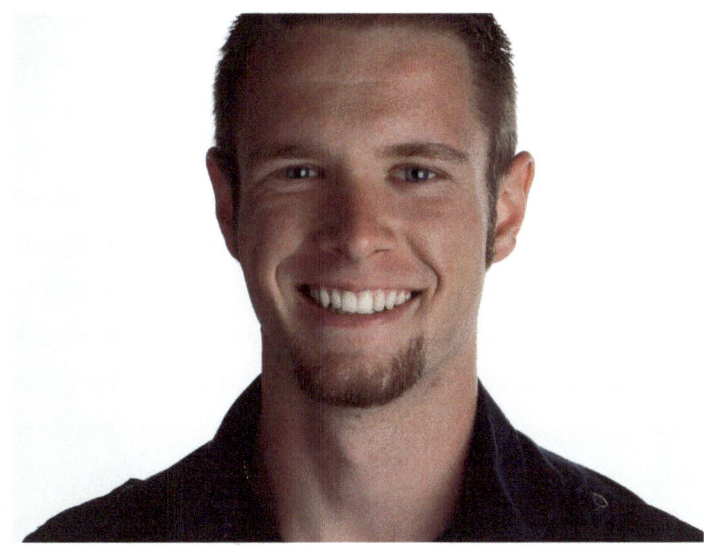

Michael Longinow
Advisor & Editor

Tamara Welter
Advisor & Chair, Journalism & Integrated Media

Nick MacNeill
Photographer & Designer

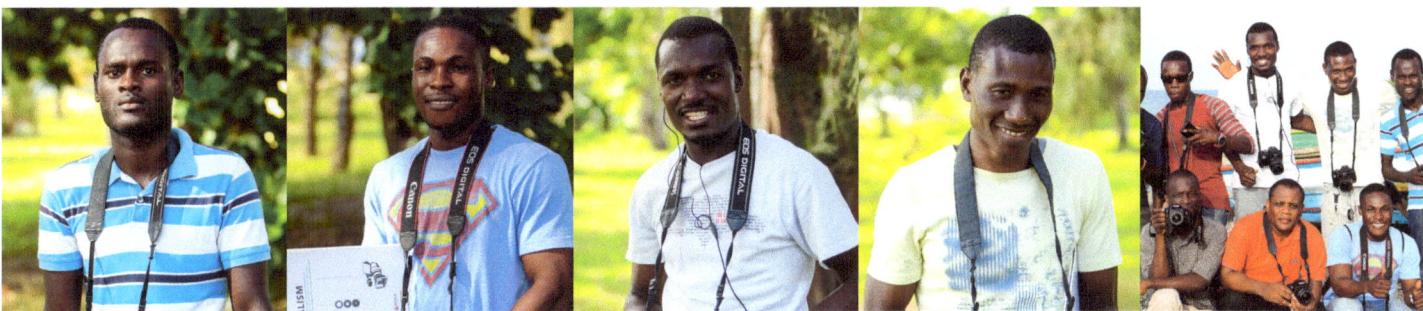

Thiery Holopherne
School Cancrab

Farchel Bertrand
School Masson

Gregory Doirin
School Leogane Guillome

Walner Joseph
School Vieux-court

www.ingramcontent.com/pod-product-compliance
Lightning Source LLC
Chambersburg PA
CBHW040756200526
45159CB00026B/2670